Music with the Under-fours

Susan Young

Routledge
Taylor & Francis Group

LONDON AND NEW YORK

First published 2003 by Routledge
2 Park Square, Milton Park, Abingdon, Oxon, OX14 4RN

Simultaneously published in the USA and Canada
by Routledge
270 Madison Ave, New York NY 10016

Routledge is an imprint of the Taylor & Francis Group

Transferred to Digital Printing 2010

Typeset in Times by
Florence Production Ltd, Stoodleigh, Devon.

British Library Cataloguing in Publication Data
A catalogue record for this book is available from the British Library

Library of Congress Cataloging in Publication Data
A catalog record for this book has been requested

ISBN 0–415–28706–5

Publisher's Note
The publisher has gone to great lengths to ensure the quality of this reprint
but points out that some imperfections in the original may be apparent.

Music with the Under-fours

The importance and value of music in the care and education of very young children is increasingly being recognised. This book looks closely at early musical development and how this translates into ways of supporting the musical activity of babies, toddlers and young children, keeping in mind the diversity of pre-school work. The following topics are included:

- Pre and postnatal musical experience;
- Music parenting;
- Lullabies and play-songs;
- Baby music sessions;
- Toddlers' music play;
- Songs, musical games and other activities;
- Young children's singing – spontaneous and joining in;
- Music play with instruments;
- Listening;
- Working with adults to develop musical opportunities.

The text provides a valuable synthesis of recent thinking in this area, as well as practical suggestions for fostering creativity through musical activities. This original and inspiring book will be welcomed by anyone responsible for the care and education of pre-school children.

Susan Young is principal lecturer in music education at the University of Surrey Roehampton.

To Michael, Ellen and Laura

Contents

Acknowledgements

I could not have written this book without the help of the many children, parents, staff, colleagues and friends who were involved in the two projects on which the book is based. I would like to thank them all. Special thanks are due to Cherry Baker, Kim Bloomfield, Margre van Gestel, Jo Glover, David Hargreaves, Maggie O'Connor, Carolyn Spencer, Alison Street, Louie Suthers and Graham Welch; to the children and staff at the early years settings which took part in the RRiF project; to Philip Trumble at the Richmond Music Trust; to Jet Davies from the Bwerani Toy Library, Kuumba Arts and Community Resources Project, Bristol; to Chris Morgan and Pat Hickman of Music and Dance in Education, Cornwall; to Sarah-Jane Wilkinson of sampad, Birmingham, and the hospital staff, and to the film crew from TV Roehampton. The RRiF Project (Roehampton and Richmond First Steps) was funded by the National Foundation for Youth Music, by Richmond EYDCP and by the University of Surrey Roehampton.

Chapter 1

Introduction

This book is the outcome of two research projects in early years music. The first focused on three- and four-year-olds in nursery settings playing with educational percussion instruments. In this first project my aim was to understand some of the processes which drive children's spontaneous musical activity and to look for ways adults might play creatively with children. This work mostly focused on instruments, as I had noticed that, while these are provided in early years settings, practitioners often feel unsure about how best they might be used. The second has been a broader project which was concerned with both research and development. It aimed to develop approaches to practice in music with under-four-year-olds in a range of early childhood settings.

It is the second project which mostly informs the book. The project was guided by questions such as: what spontaneous musical abilities do children reveal in early childhood contexts, how do they engage with musical activities which are presented to them by adults and how might adults best foster children's musicality? In order to investigate those questions I visited three early childhood settings over the course of a year for about two hours each per week. The settings were chosen to be varied yet representative. One was a nursery run as part of a family centre by social services, another was a privately funded daycare providing all-day care for babies to school-age children and the third was an Early Excellence Centre encompassing nursery education, units for children with special needs and a toy library. Kim Bloomfield, co-worker on the project, worked in music within a voluntary playgroup, in a toy library for children with special needs and at a hostel for homeless mothers.

To begin to answer the questions I started by observing, listening and writing unstructured field notes. The aim of the observations was to collect information about the settings themselves, the people who worked in them, the spontaneous musical behaviours of the children and the kinds of musical activities between adults and children which took place in these settings. It was intended to be the kind of observational information which raises questions and leads to the search for more information. After each session of observing I read back through the notebooks and used the blank pages opposite to write notes and further reflections. Through this process ideas and issues began to surface. In this way I was trying to critically analyse current practices in early childhood settings, above all my own, and to move on to produce improved versions of practice.

An important strand of this project was the observation and documentation of children's spontaneous musical behaviours. This work was underpinned by the conviction that we need to learn how to listen, to recognise and to value young children's own ways of being musical and to see these as the starting points for adults to connect with, follow and respond to. In contrast to other areas of early years practice, particularly the visual and language arts, I consider music lags behind in its collection, analysis and interpretation of young children's self-initiated activity. As a consequence, adult-led models of music practice predominate which are often, in my view, poorly connected with children's current abilities, competences and inclinations.

An outcome of the project was the making of a video which is intended to be used for training. However this also provided an unexpected, additional source of information for research as a quantity of sensitive filming of high audio and visual quality was collected by the film crew. The perceptive eyes and ears of cameraman and sound-recordist often picked out children singing in the general melee of play which I had not heard.

Central to the project was the importance of spending continuous and long periods of time in a few places in order to get to know the children and staff well, and to think about the way music might operate within the whole environment. The criteria for funding often emphasise the number of children the project will benefit, leading to the temptation for workers to scoot from setting to setting. As a result of staying long-term in a few settings, I think the project was able to evolve approaches to practice which are embedded in current practices and accord with the ways of working in those settings. For example, noticing and thinking about the very different kinds of ways coffee breaks are provided for in different settings (and the one setting with no break) may on the surface have nothing to do with the music but say much about the professional lives of the different workers and how they are viewed and view themselves. However, at the same time I am aware that what arises from and fits these settings may not transfer well to others. I would like to think, however, that it is possible to launch into more general propositions about music with under-fours from the footing of these few case studies.

An extension of the rethinking process was to spend time visiting, observing and talking to other early childhood professionals, in music and beyond. I explored a number of other projects, visited other professionals, talked to people on the phone and spent time gathering and reading descriptions and reports from other early years music projects (of which there are plenty now). I spent time in stores specialising in early childhood toys, observing parents with small children selecting and buying musical instruments, CDs and cassette players. I watched children's television shows, read the accompanying magazines and listened to CDs produced with very young children in mind.

How this book is organised

This book aims to keep in mind diverse children, diverse childhoods, diverse families, diverse settings and the diverse range of adults working with children. Yet, at the same time, it is distinctive to the area of south-west London in which I have worked and developed my ideas. While it describes practice which evolved from these contexts, I am aware that the perspectives are based on certain values and priorities which reflect my own cultural background and experiences.

The book tries not to assume that there is a 'one size fits all' approach which can transfer from setting to setting. Nor does it arrive at conclusions, or prescriptive suggestions. It aims to show how complex it all is and how thoughtful, sensitive and skilful the adults need to be. It also aims to show the wide range of skills required to work in music with under-fours and that musical skills count for only one small part in this. Indeed, it is so much part of the caring role to sing and play musically with the smallest children that formal musical skills may even get in the way by inhibiting what seems to be intuitive adult-to-child music-making.

The chapters move developmentally from pre-birth babies through to four-year-olds but dwell on key areas during individual chapters. This organisation of the chapters was chosen as much to capture the move from interdependence between infants and carers to independence and the changes in the kinds of settings within which under-fours are cared for as to emphasise developmental changes. Another natural division seems to fall between the babies and toddlers who are paired with an adult carer and the older pre-school children who are beginning to move independently into early childhood settings. Music in baby- and toddlerhood is duet music with and between adult–child pairs in many different constellations. Throughout the chapters, however, some of the key activity areas, such as singing, using instruments, media influences and so on, are common to each age phase, and to discuss them in relation to each would have become repetitive. They have either been located in the chapters where they seem to have the most relevance or, in the final two chapters, separated out into two strands.

The cut-off age for this book of around four years may seem out of step with official curriculum materials which are mostly taking the age of three as the boundary between under-threes and the Foundation Stage, three-to-fives. But this is a book which started with children and settings catering for the under-fours and is less concerned to fit in with official documentation. The rising fives move into reception classes marking a major transition point. The book's main message is music as play and adults being musically playful with children, and this version of music is *so* at odds with the way most reception classes are organised that there would have been few connecting points.

Real-life examples and descriptions drawn from observations pepper the text. They aim to ground the book and provide illustrations. They describe the embedded nature of musical activity, with toys and with other people, and model different kinds of interactions with adults, and sometimes other children. I wanted to avoid giving lists of ideas and recommendations which can be difficult to visualise in practice. They also serve to model observation and listening as fundamental to working in music with under-fours. All these descriptions are limited by the range of experiences I could gain from the project. They are primarily taken from a daycare setting because this provided the majority of the observations. Daycare also usefully gave me the opportunity to observe babies and toddlers more easily than it would have been if I had visited their homes. Some of the descriptions are drawn from the observational work of research students studying aspects of music with babies, Carolyn Spencer and Alison Street, and from the work carried out by Kim Bloomfield as part of the RRiF project. Kim's contribution of ideas, in particular her discussion and modelling of music play with her daughter Lucy at home, has been invaluable. The examples and descriptions are then commented on and lead, finally, into suggestions for practice. These practical approaches are discussed, often at some length. At the same time, background and theoretical information to inform and support practice has been provided where I thought it useful. In this way, it has been my aim to provide the deeper rationale and principles of practice rather than just the activity ideas at surface level.

Terminology

Terminology caused some problems. To refer to 'babies, toddlers and young children' may be more precise in many places than the catch-all 'children' but risked clogging up the text. Equally, 'parents, childminders, nannies, keyworkers' may be more fine-grained than 'carers' but for the same reason I chose the single term 'carers', or in other places 'practitioners', as appropriate. I hope readers will allow me some leeway with the more general terms selected for easier reading and accept that I tried to be as alert as possible to the dangers of unhelpful assumptions and divisions carried inadvertently in the choice of terms.

Chapter 2

Issues and contexts

Young children's lives are shot through with music: music in the quiet cooing of a baby in her cot; the rhythmical banging of spoon on plate; the running around singing 'Bob the Builder' more times than can be possible and tolerable; the anticipation of the 'Tickly, tickly' in a play rhyme with adults; the locked-in focus on the tinkling glass-piece mobile or boisterous dancing to a television theme tune. The sensitivity, energy and inventiveness of children's own music, and the ways they participate in and exploit the musical opportunities around them, are the starting points of this book. It is entitled, quite clearly, 'Music *with* the Under-fours' to convey the idea that music is something which happens between adults and children, and that within close and caring relationships meaningful musical development can unfold.

As more is discovered about the abilities of very young children and their positive motivation to learn, the more we realise how important it is to provide them with the best to ensure their 'well-being' now and their 'well-becoming' into the future. The purpose of this book is to contribute to an understanding of what is best, where music is concerned, for very young children. It starts from the conviction that an understanding of the processes and content of children's own musicality and music is the first priority. Then, on the basis of what we know of children's own ways of being musical and participating in music, we can think out, explore and develop models of practice. In this process I hope to be able to shift and expand notions of what music with young children might be, what it might sound like and what we might expect and aim for. There are traditions and beliefs that complicate approaches to music, and, in this process, some of these will need to be challenged.

We are in a new era of exploration and understanding of babies and toddlers. Where perhaps it was thought that babies arrived in the world with everything to learn, this idea is being turned on its head by discoveries of just how capable they are, even as newborns. Cleverly devised research is able to show that babies have early musical abilities and capacities for musical learning of which we were unaware until relatively recently. Working with children in their first years can be positively viewed as support to reinforce and extend what they can already do, rather than starting from scratch. This represents a complete turn-about from the long-held conception of the very young as incapable and with everything yet to learn.

Most of the striking achievements of the period from pre-birth to four years occur naturally when parents and caregivers play, talk, sing and dance with their children and respond well to the cues they give. Much of this book is simply about encouraging musical play among young children, and between young children and the adults who care for them. While playing together musically is natural to home and much daycare life – a majority of carers sing and jiggle with their babies and toddlers, play music in the home, in the car, buy musical toys and playthings which sound – musical play can become narrowed in pre-school settings to the more formal 'circle times'. This more formal way of including music has persisted even though it is out of keeping with the playful and interactive contexts for learning provided in most other curriculum areas.

Current contexts

In this section I will consider current contexts for early years music and how they have recently changed.

The social and economic circumstances of families with young children are changing rapidly. Demands for high-quality early years care and education for all children and for accessibility, particularly for those at risk owing to factors associated with low socioeconomic status, have become key political issues in England. A spate of government initiatives has resulted. This is a time of rapid growth in all forms of provision for early years, both in the range of opportunities for young children and in public awareness. It is an expansion, for early years music certainly, within which there are few 'benchmarks'.

The expansion is driven by awareness of the critical importance of the first years of life for all aspects of later development. Parents and carers have always instinctively used music in its many forms in children's upbringing and know how it blends across aspects of the care and education of the very young, how it envelops and benefits communication and emotional, physical and intellectual development. But there is now enough evidence emerging from research to be convincing. This doesn't mean adopting 'super-baby' approaches, accelerating development with explicit early instruction or expensive equipment. Playing Mozart daily to new-born babies, for example, certainly won't do any harm, but inappropriate interventions at too early an age may achieve very little. Careful thought needs to be given to work in music in ways which are appropriate to the very youngest children and the adults who care for them. The focus in this book is on how adults interact musically with children and set up relatively ordinary environments to support and foster musical participation and progress.

It is clear that what is best for babies and very young children is inextricably tied to their parents first, their families and communities. Parents have a more profound effect on children's learning than any kind of outside setting. If the parents employ other carers, then grandparents, childminders, nannies and daycare staff also come into the frame. As children get older, most attend early childhood settings more independently and so the net of involved adults widens. Whatever the child's network of adult carers, it is essential to find ways of starting with their expertise and integrating it with the skills and knowledge of those beyond the home. The level of facilitating and interpersonal skills required to work well with families and other caring adults cannot be overestimated.

There is a baffling diversity of provision for young children: daycare centres, home settings with childminder, social services, Sure Start, voluntary playgroups and drop-ins, toy libraries, education-run nurseries, support groups for children with special needs, and more. In one geographical area there can be hundreds of different settings where small children are gathered. To complicate the picture more the settings are run by varying agencies: voluntary, privately funded, social services, education and direct government funding. The purposes which underpin the different settings can vary widely, and the adults caring for the children bring a range of different professional roles and background training.

All these influence the nature of the experiences provided for very young children.

Increasingly music is being brought into early years settings by another group of outside agencies specifically concerned with music. These range from community musicians, health arts workers, music therapists, music educators and arts organisation professionals to independent paraprofessionals who offer workshops and sessions in music. There is growing interest among all these parties in extending their work with young children. Their motivation for doing so may vary, and the generous funding opportunities available for early years music are certainly an incentive. However, many of these agencies are still relatively inexperienced at working with under-fours and may misjudge the skills and understanding required. The important issue is that working with under-fours requires quite different and appropriately designed approaches. Scaled-down versions of the usual workshop format, children's performance or educational 'lesson' are unlikely to fit the bill. The tendency may be to fall back on tried-and-tested models of working, particularly when pressed to get work quickly up and running.

Developing dialogue

So, across the whole range of activity in music with children under four, there are professionals from a wide diversity of backgrounds working across many divisions. Who meets whom on whose terms becomes an important question. There are different ideologies and conceptions about childhood and about music, leading to varying expectations of the nature of the work and outcomes. Diversity is a potential source of strength. Exciting differences of perspective can lead to healthy cross-fertilisation and stimulating, creative approaches. The danger is that different agencies may pull in different directions, or that aims and ideals are blurred in the effort to compromise and arrive at working arrangements. At a time of initiatives and rapid change, time spent observing, listening and discussing which is built into the process becomes essential. It should be incorporated, not tokenistically but with generous, quality time and real effort. Imaginative versions of musical activity which serve the children's needs well are a positive outcome worth negotiating hard for.

It is said, all too often, that adults who have not had the benefit of some kind of training in music 'lack confidence'. The 'lack of confidence' tag is usually applied indiscriminately and within it lie many unexplored assumptions. Its consequence is to cast some adults – practitioners, parents – as the weak link and in need of training. It sees work with adults as compensatory, starting from deficits rather than looking for the competences already in place. As a result, feelings of disparity may arise which can quickly put up barriers. A more empowering and thereby productive approach is to start with assets, identify the strengths everyone brings and, in dialogue, plan the ways forward.

This is something about which I feel strongly. By spending long periods of time in early years settings as an observer and general helper I was able to see just how competently, appropriately, sensitively *and confidently* parents, carers and early years practitioners were using music in their everyday interaction with children. There are strong traditions of adults incorporating music into their upbringing of babies and very young children. Indeed, it is intuitive to the caring role to interact musically with babies (Street, 2002), and the traditions of singing to and with young children in early years settings are long established. This active music-making by women in the enclosed settings of home and nursery among small children is a genre of musical activity which has long been overlooked and devalued. The motivation to care well for young children almost always overrides any personal anxieties adults may hold about performing musically in other situations. In other words, musical insecurities are defined by the situation and what adults perceive to be its demands.

The diverse range of professionals involved in music with under-fours brings a necessary emphasis on the skills of negotiating and networking with others. The notion of 'mutuality' is a useful one. It assumes that relationships are built in which expertise is shared on a mutual basis, each contributing and learning as of need. It calls for the realisation that new possibilities will emerge from working in partnership, having faith in others and believing in their strengths. Mutuality also conveys respect for the individuality of communities, settings, practitioners, parents and the values they hold. A way of working which is appropriate in one context may not transfer to another. Within these dialogues, careful questions need to be asked about what vision of music in the future of these children do we hold? And whose vision is it – children's, parents', early childhood practitioners', educators', music professionals', policy makers', funding providers'? How best can that vision be enabled? And all this while at the same time holding on to a critical disposition and rigorously striving for the best practices. The demands are considerable but rich with possibilities.

The music of under-fours

In this section I will discuss some of the general features of music in earliest childhood.

To say that early education encompasses a rapidly changing age phase may seem to be stating the obvious, but to pause to consider the differences between a four-day-old and a four-year-old drives home the enormous transition from interdependence to independence. Working in music across this age phase requires understanding of and adapting to the developmental changes. To add to this, the children have travelled different musical paths, even the youngest babies will have heard different music in the womb, and their carers have their own musical histories to complicate the picture.

Developing motor skills, differently proportioned and smaller sized bodies, immature vocal folds, smaller lung size – all these physiological differences mean that young children's music is not simply a scaled-down version of adults'. Some adaptations are, again, too obvious to state, but others may need thinking about. A song phrasing, body movement, tempo or instrument size and hold which is comfortable for an adult may not fit the young child. On the other hand, as I will explain in Chapter 4, recent discoveries revealing the musical capabilities of young babies show that neither should we underestimate.

Music exists as a distinct art form in the minds of adults but not in the behaviour of young children. Their whole being is suffused with music. As babies they kick and vocalise in synchrony, as toddlers they sing-paint thick brush strokes of colour, they rhythm-ride push-alongs, drumming their feet on the wooden floor. Music mobilises all their senses, working together as one. It focuses all their capacities, emotional, physical, intellectual and sensory. Such multimodal learning powers the imagination and feeds into thinking in the many single-mode strands that education imposes, artificially, on children's play. That we can sift out of play vocalisations and emergent singing, rhythmic movement and making sounds with objects, and call it music, represents educational and cultural priorities to organise experience into narrowly banded areas. Nevertheless, this sifting process is valuable. It shows us the 'log-on' points for extending children's participation and learning in music.

So young children's music can sound, very often, as if it comes from different places to adults' music. It does, in a way. And music made by children, on their own or playing with adults, is often small-scale, fleeting and woven into other ongoing activity. We know to keep the scrap of sugar paper carefully dotted with red and blue ink spots, or to listen in with real effort to try and decipher the early attempts at speech. But the musical equivalents are much more difficult either to capture in the first place, to hear as music, or then to be convinced that they are valuable. This is where parents have the edge. They are usually acutely tuned in to their children and hear the cot-singing, see the knees-bend dance to music and clap along with the drumming. Music educators have tended to look for the beginnings of musical skills and processes which can lead into making music in the far-off adult future and have been less interested in learning to recognise children's music on its own terms. In contrast, art educators have a long tradition of studying young children's art and coming to understand its processes as children's art. Compare provision for the visual arts in early years with the provision for music and the effect of these differing traditions on practice is immediately apparent.

The changing musical cultures of contemporary life, and how they impinge on contemporary childhoods, also demand new thinking. In the media-rich world we have created technology can wrap us in a wealth of music all our waking hours. The listening unborn child is hearing all this and will already be familiar with music from its mother's culture at birth. This process of enculturation, absorbing from the music they hear in everyday life, continues powerfully through their early years. In this way children come to know how music from the cultures around them sounds, how it works, how people use it and respond to it. And these are not single cultures. Many children today are musically 'multicultural', and encounter many styles of music, experiencing one musical culture in the home, perhaps different music at their daycare, traditional rhymes on a grandparent's knee and pop styles in an older sibling's bedroom. These cultural experiences of music are absorbed and resurface in children's play, sometimes clearly recognisable as direct imitations or sometimes reworked and transformed beyond our capacity to recognise them.

In the permeable, technological world we now live in, information flows direct to children, bypassing the adults. Television plays an important part in children's home pre-school experience. In television programmes designed for under-fours the key characters sing for the children. Their signature songs are sung with a distinctive, often animal or pseudo-child voice. The typical style of this music, and much of the recorded music produced specifically for young children, is bright and cheerful, party music in which session musicians provide light backgrounds of primarily synthesised accompaniments. The range in terms of mood and style can be limited. The music is primarily seen as entertainment or diversion, particularly used for car journeys. There are images of children as musical and expectations of their participation in music which are held in these products.

Commercial priorities can seem to run counter to the aims and priorities of early childhood practitioners. Parents may have less time and more money for children. This, coupled with higher expectations of their achievement, is exploited in the mixed messages of 'early learning', both in the range of products and in the opportunities available. Parents receive a subtle mix of pressures to be early educators and entertainers, to provide diversion and educative experiences.

The pervasive influence of media and popular culture on children can arouse some anxiety that they are being shuttled prematurely and inappropriately towards an adult world. The response to external cultural influences is different among different groups of parents. Some may feel anxious about depriving children of appropriate stimulation, other parents may be anxious about the inroads of cultural influences and seek to insulate their children. Similar concerns can occur among early years practitioners. Many keep a clear boundary around songs and recorded music which are considered inappropriate and these are avoided or ignored. In a nursery setting I observed a singing time where one child's contribution of a current pop song was subtly passed over. There are also differences between children's popular music and adults' popular music. Most settings draw the line at any kind of inclusion of adult popular music, even though it is pervasive and children hear it all the time, but are happy for children's incorporation of popular music intended for young children. In contrast the songs selected for children to sing in pre-school settings often seem to reflect a nostalgic world of childhood, out of kilter with the realities of children's daily lives and the musics they are listening to. Thus there already begins to be a music style associated with 'school' which doesn't connect up with the music children encounter beyond. This is not emerging as an argument for 'good or bad' music – such divisions are unhelpful. Musical styles will continue to proliferate and change. Being able to slip easily between ever changing musical styles represents, as far as I can judge, a skill for future musical life. Children are extremely good at absorbing, assimilating and reworking on their own terms all that they come across. Everything is grist to their mill and, beyond ensuring as much breadth of experience as possible, I don't think we need to concern ourselves too much with the 'grist'. To continue the metaphor, it is working the mill, the ways they learn to participate, actively to work, to make their own choices and engage with the musical experiences for themselves, that will be the important skills.

Expanding ideas of musicality

In this section I will argue for a broader idea of musicality, as a set of capacities we all possess which can organise and integrate experience.

Music appears to be hard-wired in for early life. From the moment of birth, the baby can make connections with those around her through abilities which are, in many ways, fundamentally musical. These are the abilities to time well and match rhythmically with others, to shape communications with contours and variations of pitch which are expressive of emotions and to 'read' these qualities in the communications of those who care closely for her. So the 'music' made between baby and caregivers enables communication from the very start and communication forms the basis of good relating. Within an intimate relationship, the baby receives the emotional, physical and intellectual input she requires to thrive. How this communicative music works becomes only too apparent in children suffering from autistic spectrum disorders in whom the ability to read or send the musical dimension of the message is somehow blocked or closed down.

The idea that only a few people are born musical is refuted once and for all by these discoveries of musicality being fundamental to human nature. It is the experiences and opportunities children receive as they move through childhood which are the prime influences in determining how competent in music they become, not genetic inheritance. Going one stage on, if music is essential to establishing the relationship between baby and caregivers, and if this relationship is the essential raft on which later capabilities are constructed, then music is likely to play a crucial part in later development. Indeed, there is a range of emerging research which is suggesting – very tentatively as yet – that music develops capacities which are fundamental and can nourish other aspects of development. Rhythm may be the key to this.

Music happens across time: the sounds of music are organised temporally by rhythmical structures, patterns of regularity and variation. At the same time music is invisible and intangible. In order to get hold of it, mental models which can capture abstract ideas as they unfold across time have to be created. This is why language, why movement or visual representations of music often become attached and merged with the sounds. The link between time and space patterning lies behind the suggestion that experience of music – time patterning – may improve the ability to perform certain puzzles involving spatial patterning. This is the link that has been called the 'Mozart effect' (Rauscher *et al.*, 1993). This one small finding fired up enthusiasm that here was a key to making babies 'brainier'. While, as I said earlier, listening to Mozart will do no harm, the exaggerated claims of books and CD covers need to be played down. But certainly, because of its time-based and non-visual properties, music may exercise mental capacities in ways which have lasting benefits.

There are a number of studies which have found a link between increasing the amount and variety of musical experiences young children receive and improvements in other general abilities. I could quote from several but will mention one. Jordan-DeCarbo and Galliford (2001) studied the effect of a music project with 106 disadvantaged children aged from three months to four years in the United States. They found that those children who had received the music did better in some standard baseline tests for cognitive, language, motor and social-emotional skills. While many factors can influence the outcomes of studies such as these, and so we should be cautious in accepting their findings, those who carried out the study tell us that the results were striking for the short period of time the extra music was included.

However, I am not keen to promote music simply as a servant to other curriculum areas. The emphasis in education on literacy and numeracy has slipped down into the early years. Ways in which musical activities can support learning in number or language are commonly recommended in curriculum materials. In the integrated way in which children learn, activities blend across all domains and can be leaned on this way or that to develop children's understanding in single-mode areas such as number and words. But capitalising on music's flexibility in this way is to miss what it is best at. In my view, more resources and effort should be given to understanding and developing children's emotional and expressive abilities. For if these abilities are neglected, children are not even equipped to live well, let alone learn well. Multimodal, multisensorial activity is the stuff of our emotional lives, and it powers our imaginations, and our building of positive self-identities in relationship with others. Music is essentially about these things.

So music can drive in many different directions. It is fundamental to our communicating, to forming relationships, with others. It can help to regulate emotions. Music organises and energises our bodily movements. It intertwines with language, with pattern, with number and with visual imagery. Music's capacity to organise events in time seems to stimulate cognitive processes. Yet in all this it is easy to overlook the skills and understandings which are central to development and progress in music itself. These are the skills of learning to sing, of learning to play instruments, of getting better at making music up and learning to link perceptions of music with understanding of how it works, of learning more about the wealth of music made up and performed by others (see Young and Glover, 1998). The deeply rooted belief that only those who are gifted can really 'do' music reins back approaches to working in music with very young children. Music is held, implicitly, to be an add-on, a lightweight, a frill which can usefully serve other educational purposes, provide a communal occasion and some fun. Methods such as Suzuki which start children on a pathway of skill learning at precociously young ages have expectations of conformity and rote learning which clash with our notions of how children learn best. But the principle of the method, that the earliest years represent a window of opportunity, and that learning in music is as natural as learning to speak a language, rightly sets high expectations. Studies which have tracked children in music-rich homes have shown that they gain considerably from the musical environment and encouragement (e.g. Atterbury and Silcox, 1993). The challenge is to find approaches with high expectations built in which match what we know of children's musical abilities and how we think they will best improve.

Versions of musical participation

In this section I will take a broad view to consider a range of ways for engaging the under-four-year-old in musical activity. The mainstay of early childhood music practice remains the collective singing session. This way of incorporating music is drawn down into the earliest age phases with even babies, as I observed, gathered together in daycare for a circle time. In this dominant version of musical participation for the under-fours, the adult presents music and manages the activities. Workshops led by music professionals, perhaps as a one-off or short series, often follow a similar performer/audience model. Without care, such approaches may induce passivity, not only in the children but often in the adults who take part too.

Children construct their understandings through effortful interaction with people and things. The idea of musical play, of interactive music play between adults and children which, importantly, starts from the child's self-initiated activity, its own music, is much less developed. Indeed, you may, at this moment, be struggling to imagine what this might be. In comparison with other areas of play, say in art, language, construction, models of practice in early years music based on children's own self-led music are poorly developed. The youngest children are assumed to be unable to do anything for themselves without considerable help and guidance. Or, if children do make their own music, it is considered so unformed, so unlike 'real' music that it cannot constitute any kind of meaningful starting point. It's just making a noise.

In other areas – language, for example – the importance of embedding language in everyday situations and play, of adults engaging with children on their terms, have become well established. Music still seems to be taken out, separated from general play activity. Adult roles for music have tended to one of two extremes, either as leader for singing sessions or *laissez-faire*, as in free play with musical instruments. This is a sweeping generalisation, but for the most part the importance of adults interacting with children in and around the musical activities they initiate themselves is not developed in early years practice. Yet it is much more in keeping with how parents intuitively music-play with babies and toddlers. This kind of one-to-one activity is blended into everyday routines and semi-improvised, playful exchanges between adult and child. What I am suggesting is to build upwards, to construct versions of music with under-fours from those which are natural to caregiving rather than scale down the lesson, the workshop or the performance which has worked with older children.

Allowing children to take and sustain the initiative musically is key. For example, two-year-olds vocalise spontaneously and imaginatively as part of their play. The attuned adult might echo back a little snatch of the child's singing, the child hears it, and sings a further response. A small exchange like this might be over in a few seconds, but to be heard and to hear what you are producing matched by what someone else is doing is musically very powerful. The adult is offering an opportunity based on a child-led process. In this version of participation the effort to stand back, listen, focus, make sense of and adapt becomes the adult's work, rather than the child's. The possibilities for encouraging genuine musical engagement emerge from ordinary interactions, particularly when adults listen closely enough. But these are not 'show-biz' moments. The adult is making music on the child's terms; it is small-scale, often quite quiet, over in a short moment, informal, integrated into playful, everyday situations and arises from a momentary meeting of adult and child.

This is not to downplay the importance of providing a range of ways of participating. Young children gain much from being able to observe, absorb and imitate from models – when the adult sings or plays to them, for example. They may be fully engaged in listening and watching, with that wide-eyed stare, fixed to the spot, so characteristic of small children. But, in terms of actively joining in, being able to mobilise your voice and body to join in and fit in with external models is a different kind of process, and to really fit well requires considerable development of skills. If children are always being asked to adapt to given models rather than building on their own spontaneous musical contributions, it can be a frustrating process for them. It is a question of balance.

In the project which feeds into this book we started with a notion of musical experience as play-based and looking for a variety of opportunities to integrate music into general play activity. At the same time we focused on children's self-initiated ways of playing musically and sought to become more aware of them. Within such a view of music as everyday and embedded in general play activity the adult roles for music change. The adult sometimes just needs to listen, to stand back and hear the child's music, respond and comment. At other times it may be appropriate to join in and play with the children, partnering them in music play interactions. At other times the adult may take the lead, perform and model for the children. So while I don't wish to diminish the value of adult-led music – ideally to voluntary participants rather than obligatory for all – working with under-fours in music can cover a wide spectrum of adult roles. Most important, these roles are fitted around children's own ways of being musical rather than the other way round.

Child-initiated music-making raises some issues which need to be thought out carefully. The first is noise – or perhaps it is more useful to think in terms of levels of sound. There is a widespread idea that very young children's participation in music needs to be highly structured and guided. The fear is that, without this structure, their music will sound out of control and chaotic in comparison with adult versions of music. Careful listening and looking, as I will explain in later chapters, will show that there are forms of organisation and logical processes underpinning the activity. But loud, seemingly uncontrolled sounds – 'noise' – arising from music play (and I have in mind particularly with instruments and other sound-makers) can arouse anxiety among adults. It is often, incidentally, the opposite with children's spontaneous singing. Much of their singing is so quiet and unobtrusive as to go unheard altogether, although the most boisterous vocal and movement play is usually reined in. Equally exuberant play, but which is soundless, is often accommodated and tolerated more willingly and easily. Water spills out on to the floor only around the water tray, and is quickly mopped up; loud sounds spill to fill the whole room and seem to unsettle the adults around. Interestingly, I found that different settings had varying responses and unspoken rules about 'noise'. In some I could work freely without concern, in others I was very aware of sound levels. Obviously the acoustic of the building makes a big difference. But within environments intended for free play, quite clear-cut boundaries and controls on the children's freedoms are exerted.

Another issue is how to provide environments which foster music play. Early years settings provide equipment and spaces for children to engage in many different kinds of self-initiated play. Music usually isn't thought of in this way, although most settings will have a collection of percussion instruments, even if they remain mostly in a basket up on the shelf. But playthings, equipment, technology and, importantly, how these are set up in the spaces will contribute to an environment in which certain kinds of music among the children can happen. The discovery, in a daycare toddler room, that music on cassette played during the children's free play closed down their own self-initiated singing, changed the routines for when music was played and raised listening alertness to the children's own singing. The development in a nursery of semi-structured singing play areas led to quite different versions of song play with three-to-fours.

A final issue to consider is that creating an environment to foster music play is more than just a matter of equipment and how it is set out. A climate for music play includes adults who encourage imaginative activity and are not afraid of letting go. Interacting with children musically in a playful way comes very easily to most adults when it becomes just part of playing with children, as opposed to performing. On the other hand, being musically playful can feel uncomfortable when your singing, dancing or instrumental play is clearly heard or seen by other adults. Early years practitioners may be comfortable finding a child mode for talking to children, or for playing in the dough, but the musical equivalent may feel odd, at least at first. Understandably so, for ours is not a culture in which spontaneous singing, dancing and noise making of any kind, let alone children's kind, has a place, except in a few carefully prescribed situations. Important, therefore, to have the backing of a rationale for playful music practice and to have some practical strategies for getting started. For those who arrive in early years contexts with music as their expertise base, being musically playful can mean finding their usual sets of skills redundant or even getting in the way. Playing musically, like a child, can, again, feel odd for different reasons.

A climate of creativity is also about sharing emotional experiences with children, for, without stimulus, without delighting children or without sensitivity to what they are feeling, their capacities do not develop. A too instrumental view of working with children can bypass how essential it is to share pleasure. Studies of those children who go on to develop musical ability often have parents who respond enthusiastically to their efforts but at the same time work hard to support their children. There is one point of caution. The emotional level needs to be carefully judged. Over-arousal with very young children can lead to 'turn-off' or, with older children, to over-stimulation without genuine engagement.

Finally

This chapter has introduced the current situation within which many are developing their practice in music with the very youngest children and their carers. It has also described and discussed some of the overarching issues which have influenced and will thread through the chapters which follow. It is an exciting time. For as research uncovers just how musically competent young children are, and just how fundamental music is to our very nature, so this runs alongside real efforts to improve the quality of education and care for the very young. To foster music from the earliest days is being recognised as having far-reaching and important benefits. It matters a lot, then, that we do it the best we can. This is the task of the chapters which follow.

Chapter 3

Unborn and just after

This chapter will look at:

- music before birth
- music with babies needing special care
- musical communication
- infant-directed singing
- lullabies

The unborn baby is listening. Three to four months before birth, the ear is fully formed and the baby in the womb can hear (Lecanuet, 1996). Recordings made from inside the womb show that the baby hears an only slightly muffled version of everything in the mother's external world, together with the internal sounds of the mother's body. One of the first links between hearing before and after birth was the discovery that reproducing heartbeat sounds could soothe newly born babies. Hearing certain music and sounds, in particular the mother's voice, during the last few weeks of pregnancy may lead the baby to recognise and prefer them after birth. Newborns are very sensitive to their mother's voice and will recognise and turn towards it (DeCasper and Fifer, 1980). Knowing this, many suggest that it is helpful for the mother to talk reassuringly to the unborn and newly born baby.

Research has gone on to discover not only that babies are able to hear and are listening in to music before birth but that they remember and recognise this music after birth. Studies have been carried out in which the same piece of music has been played repeatedly to unborn babies. When played the same music as newborns, the babies show signs of recognising it, such as sucking more vigorously, turning their head towards the sound source or being soothed (e.g. Woodward *et al.*, 1996). In another study, they have even been shown to remember familiar music they heard in the womb as much as a year later (BBC, 2002).

Not only are the babies remembering the music, but the memory of womb music may be particularly soothing to them. A group of babies who were played lullabies daily during the nine weeks before birth cried less when newly born in comparison with a group who had not listened to the lullabies (Polverini-Rey, 1992). So mothers could be advised to sing a soothing song or lullaby frequently to their unborn child in order to have the advantage of its calming effect after birth. The idea that unborn babies are listening in – not only that, but remembering and recognising music – points to the importance of taking care of the aural environment of pregnant mothers. Researchers make it clear that they are not yet fully aware of the sensitivities of pre-natal hearing and warn that making any intrusive musical interventions, such as playing amplified music close to the womb, should be avoided. Equally, living in noisy conditions – working late into pregnancy with noisy machinery, for example – may be stressful, not just for the mother but also for the unborn child.

Music before birth

Considering all that is now known and being revealed about unborn babies' abilities, we must set back the clock and understand parental involvement and concern for the experiences and well-being of the child to begin long before birth. The idea that unborns are alert and attentive to voice, touch and music is so recent, and such a change from the usual conception of babies as unfeeling, unthinking and immobile, that it may, at first, be difficult to appreciate the value of specific music-based interventions prior to birth. Maggie O'Connor runs sessions for pregnant mothers as part of a Healing Arts unit attached to a hospital on the Isle of Wight. She includes the following kinds of activities:

•   Vocal toning (singing long vowel sounds on one continuous note) which creates internal resonances, particularly in the chest. It is relaxing both for mother and baby because it slows down the breathing.
•   Gentle singing of lullabies and other songs combined with stomach massage for relaxation.

- Individualised and made-up words to known tunes which personalise the song to a mother and her own baby. The women are encouraged to find a 'special' song for her baby and to sing it every day.
- Combined singing by the whole group which creates a listening experience for the babies in the womb.
- Partners talking and singing to the baby.
- Encouraging parents to find lullabies and baby songs which have been part of their family and community.

The benefits of these kinds of activities are many. Perhaps most valuably, through singing the babies can begin to form pre-birth relationships with their parents and parents with them. There is even beginning to be some suggestion that 'sung-to babies' show certain advances in general development and better emotional balance (Whitwell, 1999).

While pre-natal clinics and parentcraft classes have conventionally cared for the physical needs of mother and unborn child, there is now more awareness of the emotional aspects of pregnancy and the value of providing emotional support for mothers and babies. There is some evidence that stress experienced during pregnancy can be conveyed biochemically to the baby (Thurman, 1997). The birth of a new baby can be a time of stress and emotional turmoil for the mother, father and other family members. At the same time, there has been, in recent years, growing interest in the potential value of music for health and general well-being. Pregnancy and motherhood are times of evolving and changing identity, a point of transition, particularly for first-time mothers. Music-based activity can provide opportunities for expressing and dwelling on aspects of becoming a mother and helping to adjust to changes.

The generally low uptake of antenatal provision by women in the South Asian communities of Birmingham had been of concern to outreach health workers and midwives. Aware that antenatal education should reflect the diversity of women who attend, sampad, a Birmingham-based South Asian arts organisation, in partnership with the hospital antenatal services, set up culturally specific antenatal provision. Importantly for women from Muslim communities, this is a secluded, women-only environment supported by link workers who could provide translation. The work is matched to the needs, values and priorities of this minority group.

The two-hour-long sessions are attended by a sampad musician and a trainee musician playing harmonium and singing. As mothers drift in, the musician plays and sings to set a relaxed mood. The sessions move through a range of exercises involving breathing, gentle movement and relaxation and massage. The musician provides recorded South Asian 'New Age'-style music for the exercises, following the lead of the movement teacher. At other times she plays gentle drone sounds. There is time for discussion, for social contact and for concerns to be raised.

As a key part of the session, the women sing lullabies and other children's songs to their unborn children and share traditional lullabies from their varying language backgrounds: Punjabi, Urdu and Gujurati. For some of the women, many of whom are young and whose own mothers are not in Britain, it has been an opportunity to remember songs their mothers sang to them and a way of feeling connected with distant families. Songs can carry many meanings, hold many connections, and in this way can help to support life transitions – for young children no less than the mothers. Many of these women are adjusting to cultural and life-stage changes. The birthing process, traditionally supported in their culture by mothers and older women of the community, in Britain comes into the hands of medical professionals. While this assures higher standards of medical care, perhaps other qualities of care are lost. The midwives are alert to this and the classes are an attempt to redress the balance. Here is one of the traditional lullabies in Urdu sung by the women, which, translated, sings, 'Baby, baby, go to sleep. Sleep on the special red bed.'

As with any innovative project, the process of providing ample discussion time for reviewing and revising on an ongoing basis has been important. The original classes had involved dance, which some had felt was inappropriate because it was not decorous enough for Muslim women. Following this review, a second series of classes included movement work for relaxation, massage for physical well-being. The project has required collaboration between artists and health workers. Both have learnt much from each other and are beginning to incorporate new ideas into their work outside the project. Inter-agency work is challenging, as each can carry different priorities, expectations, ways of working and even ways of talking about their work.

Music with babies needing special care

In the days following birth, the external world must present a welter of auditory, visual and kinaesthetic stimulations – very much so for babies requiring intensive care. The high sensory stimulation of medical procedures, the bright lights and noises of the hospital units are stressful for premature and low-birth-weight infants, and stressful also for their parents. Recently there has been interest in music as a means to reduce the distress of fragile, premature and low-birth-weight infants, particularly in the fields of music therapy and arts-medicine. The close link between emotional state and physiological state is very clear, and music's contribution to the well-being of babies needing medical intervention has been shown in a number of research studies (e.g. Standley and Moore, 1995).

One researcher found that lullabies played to special care babies three times per day appeared to reduce the total length of hospital stay by an average of five days (Caine, 1991). In another study by Whipple (2000) parents were encouraged to use music and massage with their infants in a neonatal intensive care unit and, importantly, were taught to identify the signs of over-stimulation. The key elements of this music massage were just what might be expected:

- eye contact;
- quiet spoken voices;
- gentle touch and stroking;
- soothing, very soft rhythmic music – ideally sung;
- decrease in stimuli – dimmed lights and quietened sounds.

The babies in the music-massage group gained in weight and left hospital earlier than babies in a matching group who did not receive the music massage. This is evidence of what might be the many-sided benefits of rhythmical, musical communication through sound and touch between parents and their babies.

It stands to reason that if these benefits have been identified among premature and low-birth-weight babies, then they must also apply to all the newly born. This provides important justification for enlightening new parents about the importance of using music – both singing and appropriate recorded music – and rhythmical stroking in the care of their new babies. And, alongside this, to be alert to recognising the 'switch off' signals when babies have had enough. Health visitors have the vital role of advising and supporting newly delivered mothers. While this consists of general care of a medical nature, reflecting their health role, many are now interpreting the role more broadly. Health visitors increasingly include baby massage and baby singing in their parenting advice.

Musical communication

Listen to anyone talk to a baby and they will intuitively slip into a specific style known as infant-directed speech. They will keep to simple words, organised in short phrases which are repeated, they will speak slowly, with greater stress on certain words to make the speech more rhythmical, pause for longer than would be normal in adult speech and use an expressive 'sing-song' voice, curving up and down in pitch (H. Papousek, 1996). Successful communication with babies depends on this musical speech. The words are unimportant. The same basic characteristics of infant-directed speech are found across different cultures and different languages. Babies from the moment of birth are able to tune into these musical qualities and 'read' them in the communication. The first three postnatal months represent a period of transition to life outside the womb, and establishing good communication between parent and baby is the important work of this time.

Although usually termed 'infant-directed speech', reflecting the dominance in our culture of verbal forms of communication, 'infant-directed vocalisation' may be a more accurate term. Vocalisation can encompass the speaking voice, the singing voice and the many kinds of sing-speech which lie across the whole spectrum of voice use: crooning, humming, chanting, chirruping. Expressive voice use is just one element in a 'dance' of gestures and facial expression between caregiver and baby which conveys emotions, energies and ideas.

The musicality of communication between carer and baby has an important purpose in enabling the carer to help the baby manage its moods, emotions and physical state. Babies can live on a roller-coaster of emotions, tipping, say, from contentedness one moment into full-blown distress the next. It partly depends on the individual disposition and personality of each baby. Some are grizzly and difficult to soothe, some are quiet and not easily ruffled. But parents learn their babies' rhythms and signals and the changes in mood which they convey. The musical elements – rhythm, dynamics, pace, pitch rise and fall – in the multisensory ways carers talk, sing, hold, stroke and sway with their babies help to manage and change their babies' moods and physical state. So a distressed and fretting baby is cuddled tightly, rocked to and fro, crooned or spoken to soothingly. This emotional management is an essential part of caring for the baby, smoothing the changes of everyday routines, in and out of sleep, feeding, clothing and other care routines.

> Carolyn lifted Ben (three months) into the air, up and down gently, with a vocal 'whee-eee!' which rose up and down in pitch to match her lifting. But after a few turns she sensed his body tense and his vocal sounds became sharper. She stopped the play-game, cradled him in her left arm, rocked to and fro and talked much more quietly and soothingly to him.

Although it may appear that the caregiver is leading the inter-actions, in successful caregiver–baby interaction it is often the other way round. The adult is responding to the baby's smallest body-language, facial and vocal cues and these responses are dictating the sequence of interactions. Equally, when they have had enough, young babies will give 'turn-off' signals which caregivers learn to recognise.

At the age of around six weeks, face-to-face play interactions begin to extend. A baby who is fascinated by a parent's face and voice has a bright 'locked in' gaze. Young babies can sustain intense attention and interaction only for a short while. When they have reached over-load they may turn their head away or even shut their eyes. Parents learn what is too high and too low in terms of their own infant's arousal, but some may take longer to learn this and may over-arouse or under-arouse their babies. Parents may try to coax babies into interaction, or participation in play-songs say, in spite of the 'turn-off' signals. The gurgling, rhythmic kicking of a baby who's happily taking a turn in a conversation will become tense and jerky if the baby starts to feel stressed or overwhelmed. A session in musical communication can be an opportunity to help parents and other carers to respond confidently and sensitively, watching their babies for signals, primarily through eye contact and head turns but also through body tone, muscular tone. For every baby, the signals will differ. So in well matched, sensitive and playful communications with babies the adults adjust the amount, type and variety of stimulation the baby receives. If baby and adult make good music together, it is a vital foundation for the baby's well-being and future development.

Parenting styles vary, too, from parent to parent and among different cultural groups. Although key features of infant-directed vocalisation have been found to be common across many cultural groups, conventions and traditions influence styles of caregiving and playing with babies.

Infant-directed singing

In an interesting experiment, adults were asked to sing a song 'as if' to a baby and then 'normally'. What this study found was that, when singing 'as if', the adults sang in a higher pitch, at a slower tempo, with a more loving tone of voice and that they put longer pauses between phrases than in the versions when they were not singing to infants (Trainor, 1996). In turn, babies preferred infant-directed singing to non-infant-directed singing. ID speech and ID singing (to use the short-hand terms) share most of the same characteristics. This stands to reason. But it is interesting to find that the universal features of adult communication to babies instinctively seep into singing as well. What is even more interesting is that babies seem to listen attentively to their mothers singing to them for a longer time than they will listen to their mothers talking to them.

Alison Street (2002) is questioning mothers about singing to their babies. Her work is finding that almost without exception mothers sing to their babies, that they have a special repertoire of songs for baby and that they recognise that their singing has important benefits. Her work is beginning to suggest that singing:

• is a special focused time that helps build the relationship between mother and baby;
• helps mothers to understand and respond appropriately to baby's nonverbal cues;

- promotes feelings of competence and confidence in caring for baby;
- improves mother–infant communication;
- increases mothers' ability to help their babies relax in times of stress.

Singing is a moment of intimacy, a concentrated bonding time when interaction between baby and adult is very focused. So singing can help mothers to build strong, nurturing relationships with their babies. A baby's early attachment to a parent or carer is essential if he or she is to develop a secure sense of self and emotional balance.

Karen MacKenzie (2002) also quizzed mothers about singing to their babies but from her answers found that many mothers use recorded music and that singing while driving the car was very common, even to quite young babies. She decided that contemporary life brings different kinds of caregiving routines and that mothers singing on their own, face-to-face with babies, may be less common than we tend to think. Her slightly different slant on mother–baby singing shows that we still have much to find out.

Singing may act as stress relief for parents and help them to feel closer to baby. If mothers in particular can feel they are relieving their child's distress then this will boost their confidence, helping them to feel positive about their relationship with their baby. The baby may well react to the mother's heightened sense of well-being and this may, in a positive cycle, help the baby relax and feel at ease (Oldfield and Bunce, 2001). Mothers who have difficulty in bonding with their babies, such as those with depression or those who are very young, or displaced in some way, may find musical activity, such as rocking, moving to music, singing lullabies, help to provide a focus and structure for their interactions. Experiments to test whether mothers' singing had any direct effect on six-month-old babies' stress levels by measuring cortisol levels in the babies' saliva have shown that singing does make a small difference. Those babies who were at a low level of arousal showed a rise, and vice versa (Shenfield, Trehub and Nakata, in press). So singing to babies may be a particularly useful strategy for helping mother-and-baby pairs to knit their emotional lives together.

Most of the work on singing to babies focuses on mothers. This is not to overlook the importance and value of fathers, grandparents, older siblings or other close carers singing to babies.

Soothing and settling

Lulling a baby to sleep with singing is an age-old part of child care. More than just calming, many mothers report that they sing to their babies in a particular kind of way in order to settle, to help them unwind as a preparation for sleep or for other activities. One mother said she sometimes sings her particular lullaby 'oh, a hundred times over, it's a kind of meditation, I suppose' (Spencer, 2000). By this she shows how, in the first months, the parent has an important role in managing the baby's emotions.

Lara remembered that with her first child she had repeatedly sung 'The water is wide', an English folk song which she had heard and learnt from the 1960s folk song revivalist Joan Baez. Like many of the songs sung to babies, it came from her own repertoire of songs which she had heard from the recorded version, liked and remembered, and which seemed well suited to singing to her child. With her second child a low-pitched, hummed drone combined with a gentle stroking motion had been the most effective for settling her to sleep.

In a short series of informal interviews as part of the project upon which much of this book is based, many parents talked of singing the 'most unbaby-like songs' to their children. Peter liked to sing 'Lonesome Road' by James Taylor to settle his twin baby sons and drew upon his wider repertoire of jazz favourites if the singing extended on for longer. Since research has shown that we instinctively sing in a certain way to babies, the way the song is sung is much more important than which song is chosen for the purpose. Baby Maia has come to expect a repertoire of bedtime songs from Chris, but he must sing them in a whisper because she is too stimulated by his full-voiced singing. Because the song is also soothing to the parent, choosing a song which is meaningful to the parent as well, and says something about their own identity, before, now with the baby and into the future of the child, is also important. Ayisha sings an Arabic lullaby to Mohammed which her mother, in turn, had sung to her. The arrival of a baby is a meeting point of generations, of times before and after, in songs no less.

Rachel cares for three-month to one-year-old babies in a day-care centre and her favourite song for sleep time is the Bangles'

'Close your eyes'. When I watch she has nestled two of her babies either side of her on the floor with cushions and blankets so that she can give soothing strokes to each baby as she sings.

There is a wide range of song forms which can serve as soothers. They include:

- special songs with a clear text 'sleep, baby sleep';
- traditional folk songs and nursery rhymes of a more general nature which are soothingly sung;
- improvisations by the mother in which the text is not so special – humming, syllable sounds such as 'doo, dum di dum';
- improvisations by the mother which address the baby, spontaneous ditties which are often expressive of her bonding with the baby;
- songs adapted by the mother, often popular songs, or improvisations which are more expressive of the mother's feelings in relation to the baby, fears and hopes.

Recorded music may be specially chosen because it is soothing, tapes and CDs with selections of music for relaxation or meditation, for example. And equipment is available which repeatedly plays natural sounds such as running streams, waves and the wind in forest trees. These sounds can be useful, particularly as background, but are a poor substitute for infant-directed singing and human contact.

Lullabies

> Listen to the tree bear
> Crying in the night,
> Crying for his mammy
> In the pale moonlight.
>
> What will his mammy do
> When she hears him cry?
> She'll tuck him in a cocoa pod
> And sing a lullaby.
>> (Traditional African, in Foster and Thompson, 1996: 27)

Trehub and Schellenberg (1993) researched the use and characteristics of traditional lullabies sung to babies and young children. They suggest that across cultures they share certain features:

- are softly sung;
- slow in tempo;
- usually quite short;
- sung on a limited number of pitches;
- across a narrow pitch range;
- have simple, repeated melodic ideas;
- often freely sung and semi-improvised;
- have humming and syllable sounds ('lulla, lullay') as well as words;
- contain rhythmic features linked with rocking and swaying movements;
- are addressed to the baby, include their name and have words of affection;

and continue indefinitely until the baby is quiet or asleep.

In this traditional lullaby from Shetland the crooning sounds, 'baloo, balili,' rock the baby, the bairn, to sleep.

Lullabies are often expressive of the parents' dreams for the baby's future, their circumstances, responsibilities and worries. Traditional lullabies, particularly of industrial working classes, reflect the poverty and harsh conditions of many families with young children.

Hush-a-bye baby, lie still, lie still.
Your mother has gone to the mill, the mill.
Baby's not sleeping for want of good keeping.
Hush-a-bye baby, lie still, lie still.

Bodily contact and movement

When parents or carers sing to babies to soothe and bond with them, they instinctively hug, cradle, rock and stroke them. Being carried and swayed in time to music is very pleasurable to babies, enabling them to experience movement they cannot yet achieve alone. Bodily contact and rhythmical movement are unified with singing, as one multisensory experience. The carer will automatically rock or stroke in time with the pulse and phrasing of the song. The upsurge of interest in baby massage has linked with the increased realisation of the value of singing and music to babies. As a consequence, many parentcraft classes combine the two. Needless to say, massage requires specific instruction.

Almost any recorded music which captures the mood of calm relaxation is appropriate for soothing, massage and rocking times: baroque, calming classical, classical Indian music, meditation music, children's lullabies. Much New Age music with its incorporation of actual or simulated natural sounds, its drones and meditative slow-moving melodies seeks to create these moods.

Finally

Some express concern that traditions of singing to, playing with and cradling babies are diminishing with contemporary lifestyles – that parents don't have time, they leave babies in automatic rockers with cassette music to listen to and that they no longer know a common repertoire of lullabies. Recorded versions of music are no substitute for singing to babies, with its complete package of physical contact, mutual gazing, responsive timing and rhythmical movement. And there are the many broader benefits in terms of attachment and early development which can be supported by communicating musically and making music with very young babies. The question of knowing lullabies and baby songs seems relatively unimportant, since it is the way the song is sung – not what song – which matters. But helping parents to recall a traditional repertoire of lullabies and play-songs may be a helpful starting point to singing with their babies for some. At the same time, we should be mindful that adding to the parents' burdens of 'ought to do' things may be counterproductive.

Chapter 4

The first year

This chapter will look at:

- early musical abilities
- music between adults and babies in daycare
- playing musically with babies
- baby play-songs and rhymes
- baby music stuff

In the previous chapter we saw how music – or more specifically the musicality of communication – is at the heart of early development. This musicality is the means by which babies form stable relationships with others and thus ensure they survive and thrive (Trevarthen, 1980). In the first year of babyhood the earliest interactions which are so importantly established through vocalisation, bodily contact, facial expression and gesture are continued and extend into more elaborated games and play-songs. We saw that it was not *what* is said, sung or game-played but *how*, and that the musical qualities and their non-verbal communicative possibilities are the key to successful early interaction. The baby is then, subtly, in charge, training the parent to provide it with all it needs – to help regulate its emotions, organise its physical self, provide information and entertainment. When children experience more varied activities with high parental involvement, affectionately and sensitively given, it bodes well for their future social and cognitive development.

Today's children are born into a musically rich world: richer than ever before. At the touch of a button, in the house or in the car, music from all over the world and from almost any time past can be ours. Beyond the home there is music we may not have chosen, in shops, waiting rooms, restaurants and travel termini. The child hears this musical world too, it wraps around us all. So in their first year babies are continually soaking up from everyday listening much more music than any previous generation and music of much more variety. Parents also provide music for them to listen to: cot mobiles, activity units, soothers and children's CDs and videos. The idea of entertaining children with commercial products already takes a hold, even with babies. Somehow the image of babies being content to listen to music and stay happily in their cots for longer seems to underlie many of these products. Baby stuff catalogues show Baby playing happily alone, freeing up the parents.

But it is also a noisy world. Contemporary life is full of sounds which can be confusing and overloading to a very young child: the television, CD player, home machinery, buzzers and bleepers and traffic noise of all kinds. Taking care of the audible environment, and ensuring at least some periods of quiet, helps listening, particularly listening perceptively. There is a risk that small children may learn to close down attentive listening in order to survive the aural overload. This may be particularly so in homes where the television is left constantly switched on.

Early musical abilities

Understandably, investigating the musical abilities of babies is not straightforward and requires special techniques. As researchers become more experienced at devising and using these techniques they are discovering that babies are far more able, musically, than had ever before been imagined.

A number of ingenious tests have shown that babies are very capable listeners and that they can discriminate finely between the different sounds they hear (Trehub and Trainor, 1993). For example, five-month-olds could distinguish between two pitches very close together, the difference between them being even smaller than the semitone interval on a conventional keyboard. Babies a few months older are able to tell when melodies have been altered in small ways, showing that, like adults, they remember the overall contour of the melody rather than hearing it as just a series of separate pitches (Trehub et al., 1984). Similarly, they are not deterred from recognising a melody as the same if it is played at a faster or slower speed. Another set of experiments suggested that babies even remember the actual pitch that a short melody is played at, quickly losing interest in the same-pitch version but being interested in a changed-pitch version (Saffran and Griepentrog, 2001). Of course, these laboratory experiments isolate single musical elements in an artificial way which is quite unlike everyday musical experience. But, collectively, they show that in their first year babies are highly sensitive to pitch and to the way that musical pitch and rhythm are organised into phrases. This sensitivity is essential to the baby if it is to perceive the small changes and variations in the communication 'music' it makes with its closest carers.

These fine-grained aural abilities are also essential to babies in learning to distinguish and reproduce the individual spoken sounds, the phonemes, of their language. At the same time, aurally alert babies must be well tuned in to and soaking up the detail of music they hear around them. It suggests that the earliest years are a critical period when musical abilities are primed and ready. It is our responsibility as adults to provide the quality musical experiences that take best advantage of this time. But, as the next section will show, making music with babies in their first year does not require special interventions, it is tied into everyday and ordinary playing together.

Music between adults and babies in daycare

The following observations are gathered from daycare. This is a more accessible environment in which to observe babies and carers than the home but they are typical of everyday, one-to-one interaction between carer baby pairs in any setting. In this daycare, usually around six to eight babies aged three months to eighteen months were cared for in one large room with play, sleep, changing and eating areas provided in separate corners.

> Rosie (five months) is newly arrived at daycare. She is sitting in the crook of her key worker's knee. Lena is playing with her one-to-one, improvising a little playful tickling game – 'Ticky, ticky, ticky, TICK!' Tickly fingers run up Rosie's leg to catch her toes. Lena repeats this tiny game many times. Rosie begins to anticipate the tickling of her toes and draws up her knees in excited expectation.

The youngest babies, when wakeful and alert, want the contact and attention of adults; they are not yet interested in playing for any focused period of time with toys. They enjoy little playful games which involve rhythmical words, often nonsense sounds, touching and eye contact. Lena's voice pitch rises to the final 'tick'. Rosie quickly learns its rhythmical pattern and to anticipate its phrasing.

> Flora (eleven months) bounces up and down on a blow-up floor cushion and goes, 'Er, er, er' and 'Mmmmm . . .' rhythmically as she bounces. This is unusually loud and energetic, and it attracts everyone's attention.
> Di from across the room says, 'Bouncy, bouncy, Flora, are you bouncing up and down?' in imitation of her movement and vocalisation. Di looks over and smiles at her.
> Flora's key worker, Rachel, is sitting in a chair feeding Tyler, but shuffles closer and chants to Flora, 'Bouncy, bouncy, up and down, Bouncy, bouncy, off to town' (the first two lines of a knee-bouncing rhyme they often say and do with the children). She looks at Tyler. 'Bouncy, bouncy,' she says to him, much more slowly, with a different kind of tone.

It can be difficult for key workers with responsibility for up to three babies – or for a mother with a baby and a toddler – to interact with and to co-ordinate their care and attention with more than one. Here Flora's key worker had left her to play sitting up in a blow-up support on the floor with a range of small hand-held toys. Flora's movement and vocalisation play were picked up first by another adult across the room and this brought it to the attention of Rachel, who linked it with one of the rhymes Flora would have heard before. She switched her attention back to the baby she was feeding and successfully co-ordinated her attention to both children at the same time.

Flora's moment of fun and excitement rippled through the room and the practitioners were alert to picking up, almost intuitively, cues from the children's play and responding to them. Thinking in purely musical terms, Flora's rhythmic movement and vocalisations were positively noticed and added to, and the fun was shared.

> Jake (twelve months) is newly upright and can toddle unsteadily around the nursery room with the support of the low-height equipment. He taps energetically and regularly with both hands together on a table surface. He then transfers the

same movement to a partition wall. Here his banging produces a much louder resonant noise. He pauses, continues, always tapping at exactly the same pace. He pauses and continues a few more times.

Di is concerned that the next-door room will be disturbed by his banging and so finds him a drum. 'Here, Jake, try banging on this, see how this sounds.' She taps it for him to listen. He watches. Although not easily dissuaded from banging on the wall, Jake is successfully diverted to the drum. Di searches for some more interesting objects to bang—a plastic bin, the washing-up bowl, a tin from the treasure basket are all assembled for him to tap.

A steady, rhythmic tapping with both hands simultaneously in short bursts followed by pauses is often one of the first movements applied to objects, both as a movement pattern and for interest in the sound which is produced. Here the practitioner extended Jake's activity by finding objects which produced a variety of sounds when struck and successfully diverted him into an activity which no longer disturbed the room next door.

These descriptions demonstrate how much spontaneous play is focused on rhythmical movement, vocalisations and forms of patterning and phrasing. They also show how adults can connect and interact with children on the same terms; structuring interactions around playful rhymes, empathising and taking pleasure in the babies' actions and vocalisations.

Whether among family members or other primary caregivers, playing musically with babies and young children can help adults to be playful in ways which are appropriate to the babies' current priorities and to have affectionate fun together. What I hope to have captured in the brief descriptions above is the intimacy of these exchanges—small moments of caring for the emotional well-being of the babies. There is some evidence that babies and toddlers who are enrolled in daycare with more responsive caregivers are likely to have better cognitive and language development and to be more competent socially (Goldschmied and Jackson, 1994).

In all these observations it is clear that the baby initiates the activity. Even little Rosie, sitting in the crook of Lena's knee, will have signalled her readiness to play and will have given positive cues to Lena's first introduction of a game. Whether the babies respond or initiate is less important than that each partner in the game is responsive to the other, so that the lead subtly shifts. Adults should in no way cajole or persuade babies into musical activities they are not ready for.

Playing musically with babies

As babies get older, adults bring more complex patterns of play-songs, rhymes and action games into their play with them (M. Papousek, 1996). These play patterns have certain features which help the babies to engage with adults. The play is often structured around game formats which include anticipation, surprise, teases, having fun and laughing. The games typically contain repetitions which increase little by little to a point of climax. The game-rhyme, 'Round and round the garden, like a teddy bear – one step, two steps, tickly under there!' is known to most. In itself it rises up to a point of tension and climax at the 'tickly' under there. This is quickly understood by the child, who learns to expect the final tickle. The game will be repeated many times. At first the adult probably repeats the rhyme at much the same pace, but subsequent repetitions will vary – perhaps one drags slowly, another dashes suddenly, another accelerates. These variations are carefully judged by the adult to provide just enough variation within what is familiar. In this way, stimulation and interest are measured out in doses the baby can cope with. Importantly the baby's experiences are neither rigidly unchanging nor randomly ever-changing.

The features of music play with babies

Pitch

As explained in Chapter 2, the pitch of infant-directed vocalising (speech and singing) is usually higher than vocalising which is not infant-directed. But singing for babies seems to vary in pitch. Some groups of carers and babies I have observed seem automatically to sing in low pitch, a kind of croon. Whether the pitch of singing to babies is high or low seems to depend on various factors:

- *The emotional content of the song.* Is it an up-winder, which tends to be sung in higher, rising and more animated style, or a down-winder, which tends to be sung in a falling, soothing style?

- *The age of the babies/toddlers.* Younger babies may be less tolerant of stimulating, higher-pitched singing experiences than older ones.
- *The confidence of the adult singers, the context.* Adults unsure of their singing voice in certain situations may tend – or prefer – to sing at a lower pitch.
- *The parenting style.* Preferring to animate or soothe may reflect cultural or personal parenting styles.

Pace

Generally the pace is slowed right down. The weight of the baby or toddler in the carer's arms for lifting and swinging activities may influence the pace of musical activities. Heavier babies might be heavy to lift into the air, some may enjoy the speed, some may dislike it very much.

Some older babies will be mobile in some way: shuffling, crawling or just toddling upright if supported. These babies will enjoy a pace of songs, rhymes or other music which matches their new-found mobility.

Phrasing

The phrasing of speech often follows exaggerated contours – the characteristic 'sing-song' voice in which adults speak to babies. But, again, the phrasing of lullabies and play-songs may be quite short in length, and quite narrow in pitch range. Longer pauses at the ends of phrases will enable the baby to engage in some way and to offer its turn by a vocalisation or movement.

Structure

The structure of baby songs is generally simple and well defined. Direction, anticipation to a point of climax and then some kind of resolution within a short structure is the usual. Setting this up so that the child can learn what to expect and then thwarting the expectation creates added challenge and stimulus. The aim is to create a balance between predictability and variation. The adult matches her input to what she senses the child needs and can cope with.

Repetition

Repetition of words, of musical ideas such as short melodic phrases, rhythmic patterns, claps and tapping, repetition of game movements, all allow babies to predict, anticipate and thereby to engage with the activity. They can exert control by their responses and participation.

Dynamic

With babies some advocate a very calm, quiet, low-key atmosphere to avoid anything with a sudden energy to it which may alarm. Again it probably depends on many factors, and should be judged in relation to individual babies and individual groups of babies and carers.

Frameworking

Song singing and music play feed into the relationship between carer and child by providing a framework for communicating, sharing and playing together. Musical activity may be able to support aspects of relating more successfully than just speaking to babies.

One mother said, 'When my baby was very young it was sometimes hard to talk him for longer periods of time and I found singing was easier. It gives a fixed set of words, to sort of carry you along.' She said it also felt softer and more gentle to sing than to speak to her baby.

It may help carers to use their voice and face more expressively and convey their feelings more clearly (Oldfield and Bunce, 2001), again useful for all carers but particularly so for those who are experiencing difficulty in relating. On the flip side, the relationship between carer and child can provide a frame for musical activity, for hearing a lot more songs and rhymes, with their richness of melody and language, for receiving the rhythmic stimulus of movement games, for experiencing variations of musical elements such as pace and dynamics.

If the baby's vocalisations, sound-making and rhythmic movement are warmly received and responded to with enthusiasm, this lays positive foundations for later musical development. If they are closed down, responded to as irksome, too noisy or over-boisterous, this may have a long-lasting detrimental effect on the child's musical self-identity. To look back to one of the examples, Jake could have been told to stop his banging but instead it was productively diverted.

Mothers and babies with special needs

Singing to babies and the playful patterns of game songs can provide ready-made frameworks to support interaction between mothers and their babies who are experiencing particular difficulties in communicating in a well matched way. The difficulties may have emotional and/or physical causes.

Postnatal depression occurs at a sensitive time for the developing relationship between mother and child. Mothers who suffer from postnatal depression often experience some sort of interactive difficulty with their babies and for the babies there is an increased risk of poor emotional adjustment. Very young mothers may have emotional needs of their own which are put under extra strain by the arrival of a new baby. Parents of blind infants find it more difficult to read subtle emotional signals carried in the visual expressions of their infants and to incorporate objects into play smoothly, owing to lack of eye gaze direction as a cue to emotional expression and attention. For the visually impaired mothers of sighted infants there will be similar difficulties in reading visual cues but voice and touch both provide a rich resource for successful relating.

Baby play-songs and rhymes

Play-songs

Play-songs have a different character from lullabies in that the aim is to arouse and amuse. In comparison with lullabies, the characteristics of play-songs are:

- a faster tempo;
- a wider pitch range;
- an animated style;
- the words are more important, often key to the song;

- the rhythms are more closely linked with the words than with rocking movements;
- gestures are often included, to illustrate the words;
- they increasingly involve active participation with the baby as it becomes older;
- they can have some kind of educative purpose – such as teaching parts of the body, counting, etc.

(Trehub and Schellenberg, 1995)

Children enjoy physical activity with their parents or carers; sitting on their laps, on the floor between their knees, being gripped in both hands and lifted into the air. Babies' personalities and disposition for energetic or gentle movement will vary, as will their current mood and level of wakefulness. The physical contact and experience of being bounced, carried and lifted provide them with multisensory experiences in which sound, touch and physical movement are unified.

Finger-plays and toe-plays

Tommy, Tommy,
Tommy, Tommy,
Whoops, Tommy.
Whoops, Tommy.
Tommy, Tommy,
Tommy.

Gently pinch the end of each finger in turn, starting with the little finger. Do this quite slowly and say 'Tommy' for each finger. On the 'Whoops', slide down the index finger and up the thumb. Pinch the thumb on 'Tommy' and then do the whole rhyme in reverse.

Tickling and teasing

Round and round the garden
Like a teddy bear:
One step,
Two steps,
And tickly under there!

Rocking and swinging

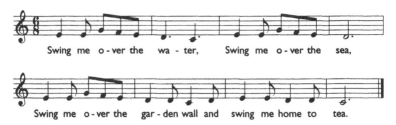

Swing me o-ver the wa-ter,   Swing me o-ver the sea,

Swing me o-ver the gar-den wall and swing me home to tea.

Lap bouncing and jogging

The newly-standing or those who are practising their upright balancing enjoy being held upright on a lap. On the final 'wow, wow, wow', swing baby up and down or twirl around.

Ri-ding on my po-ny, my po-ny, my po-ny.

Ri-ding on my po-ny, wow, wow, wow!

Moving and dancing songs

> Fly baby, fly
> Up, up so high.
> Fly baby, fly
> Right up to the sky.
> Wheeeeeee !
>   (Larkin and Suthers, 2000)

The babies can be carried on the hip, or given rides, piggy-back or piggy 'front'. The adult walks, jogs, gallops, dances. Or they can move the babies around with lifts and swings.

- Baby and carer face one another – the baby is gripped under the arms and lifted aloft.
- Baby and carer face the same way – the adult carer holds the baby under her armpits, locked on to her chest, legs dangling, swinging to and fro.
- Baby is held in a 'learning to swim' position – one arm between the legs, the other across the chest, for aeroplane swings or floating movements.

Songs and rhymes for care routines

Some babies find the usual care routines such as bathtime and nappy changing very stressful and will tend to cry and show other physical responses such as arching their back and jerking their limbs.

Scrub your dirty hands,
Scrub your dirty hands,
With a rub, dub, dub and a rub, dub, dub,
Scrub your dirty hands.

All kinds of variations of this simple rhyme can be invented to fit with activities. The rhyme can turn into a song with an improvised melody, just made up on the spot. Another way of turning rhymes into made-up songs is to start with the tune of a known song. Take, for example, the melody of 'Ring-a, ring-a roses' and let the made-up version flow on from this starting point.

Bedtime songs

The tradition of lullabies continues and as babies become older can develop into a routine of bedtime songs and rhymes. With the addition of a song or rhyme book, book reading and song singing become integrated as one. There are many crossovers between the two areas of book reading, literacy and language development and rhyme-song singing.

Baby music stuff

Striking in the direction of suspended or proffered toys is usually the first movement babies achieve at around three months and more. Sound-makers are strung across or suspended over child seats and cots. Babies enjoy mobiles, and these can be made of all kinds of materials, providing both visual and aural stimulation: suspended clusters of shiny bells, translucent shells, coloured pottery shapes, metal pieces or bamboo. Young babies can be supported or lifted up to swipe, listen, watch and enjoy together with their carer.

Rattles are almost the first sound-maker as soon as the baby can clasp. Many small rattles are available to buy but they vary considerably in the kind and quality of sound. It is worth listening to them very carefully when choosing.

Babies are interested both in the sound itself, the timbre of instruments and sound-makers, and in the physical actions required to produce the sounds. They listen with an intent, locked-in concentration. At around five months they can grip rattles and look at them, shaking them with the characteristic, slightly jerky movements of that age. The usual pattern is to shake in short bursts of regular movements, then pause, then again. They may drop and lose them and not know where they have gone. For children who are crawling there are a number of push-along or pull-along rattles and things which roll and jingle.

Emma (eleven months) pushes a wheel-like bell rattle across the smooth floor of the kitchen, watches and listens to it go, then crawls after it to repeat the same action. I watch her repeat the activity six times over.

Children's dancing and rhythmical movement can be enhanced by equipment such as swings, trampolines, slides, outdoor play equipment, bouncy cushions and blow-ups. We saw, in the observations, how Flora found a movement and vocal idea from sitting on a bouncy cushion. Children's own movements can be stimulated by equipment which motivates movement or is suggestive of movement styles, such as parachutes, bubbles, lightweight fabrics, puppets and toys.

Treasure baskets

Many early childhood practitioners will be familiar with the term 'treasure baskets' coined by Elinor Goldshmied (Goldschmied and Jackson, 1994) and used to describe baskets filled with an assortment of natural, everyday found objects such as corks, pieces of chain, shells and so on with which the babies can play freely.

Max (eight months) was sitting on the floor playing with a piece of heavy-duty steel chain, one of the items from a treasure basket of sound-makers – lifting it and dropping it on to a plastic play surface, enjoying its tactile, visual and aural qualities – the weight, the cold smoothness, the way it changed shape as the links moved and the clattering jangle it made.

Music treasure baskets can contain a variety of sound-makers. Many found items will tap, shake and rattle to produce interesting sounds. Suggestions for items include small wooden shakers or egg shakers, wooden rattles, metal chain available from hardware stores, metal dishes and spoons, strings of nutshells of the kind available from music equipment suppliers – all safe, washable and wipable.

Finally

Music with babies is essentially about understanding how simple it all is. It needs no special CDs, or television programmes, or equipment, or sessions led by those with formal musical training. Most important, babies will make music with those who are close and familiar to them as part of affectionate, everyday playful activity. At heart, music with babies is about recognising the value and importance of what might seem, otherwise, relatively ordinary and understated. Noticing, feeding back and validating what many carers were already doing and discussing it with them to develop a rationale to continue and do more of it became my role in the project rather than taking over the music-making role myself.

Chapter 5

Music with toddlers

This chapter will look at:

- spontaneous music play
- adults responding to spontaneous music play
- everyday music
- providing a song-rich environment
- providing an environment for play with sound-makers

Toddlers like to do all the things we call music and they do them of their own will, weaving them into their everyday play with the things and people around them. They spontaneously vocalise, sing, reproduce songs they have heard, play with words, dance, listen intently to sounds and music, respond to music played by others, find interesting sounds to make and organise their tapping or striking into regularities and patterns. This chapter will describe the nature of spontaneous musical play among toddlers – I have in mind roughly the age phase from one year to two and a half years old – and discuss the adult roles which fit with their play. The improvisational music–dance–game playing which we saw was so central to the carer–baby relationship continues on into toddlerhood and is an important influence on the adult role.

For the toddler, the abilities to name and to walk occur at about the same time. These newly acquired abilities open up huge possibilities to explore and interact with the surrounding environment. The overwhelming need to play with and discover the potential of all that is around them, their spontaneity and unpredictability, can create new demands on the adults who care for them. Just how do adults move in and around that? But close and thoughtful observation can show that there are forms of organisation and continuities in their play which make sense on the children's terms. Toddlers are taking what they need from their surroundings, appropriating it and transforming it for their own purposes. The adults become ports of call, offering resources, stimulation in well judged amounts, sensitive responsiveness, acceptance, reassurance and encouragement. At this age, for those children who have been parented 'well enough', there is a continual tug between the need for attachment and the need for exploration. Young children still want to stay within close range of trusted adults and refer back for reassurance. Music happens with familiar adults on laps or staying close by. Yet at the same time toddlers' curiosity and drive to find out draws them away and closer to sources of interest.

As their ability to express themselves in words develops it evolves as just one part of a mosaic of expressive, imaginative vocalisations which toddlers blend into their playful communication with others, their body-movement play and play with toys. Learning to use language and learning to sing are two important and intertwined strands of activity which emerge from vocal play, but a division between singing and speaking can mask the broad range of this play and how it connects with other areas of activity. It can also narrowly define the use of rhymes and songs in early years practice to the service of language development, distracting attention from toddlers' singing of itself and from the creative expressiveness and exuberant fantasy of their vocal play.

This is also a time of rapid development in physical skills. Toddlers are up on their feet and away. The characteristic toddle, with its unsteady rhythms, soon gives way to more assured balances, co-ordinations and mobilities. At the same time, finer motor skills develop. Toddlers will focus intently on handling and fingering small details which take their attention. The shapes and rhythms of their movement encompass this range from large-scale energies of whole-body movement to the finest, tiny fingerings.

Children's sense of themselves as musical is already being formed through their interactions with adults. Those children who see adults being actively musical will begin to absorb and imitate this. In our culture, active, participatory music-making is not commonly part of adult life. In other cultures it may be more so. In Cyprus I joined in an informal evening of dancing and music, a fusion of traditional folk with disco styles, and as in many Mediterranean countries the toddlers were not excluded from what might elsewhere be reserved as an adult space and time. They watched, or took part, or were carried as dancing partners. Being taken seriously as musical when spontaneously singing, playing instruments or dancing will feed back into their musical self-identity.

Spontaneous music play

Young children's musicality is embedded in general play, but strands of activity which we call 'musical' can be drawn out. It can be categorised into general areas of musical activity – rhythmical movement, use of the voice, play with sound-makers and interest in listening. However, beneath the surface of the activities may be generic cognitive processes which support musicality, but which, I suggest, are also connectors with learning and development in other areas.

Musical activities

Vocal play

In Chapter 7 I will describe in detail spontaneous vocal play among children of three to four years old, for this was the age phase in which I noticed it was the most prolific. But from listening to and observing one- to two-year-olds I have many instances of emerging versions of spontaneous vocal play collected in the observation notes:

- vocalising with own movement or the movement of toys;
- making sounds to animate toys;
- singing snatches of songs and reworking them in play;
- vocalising repetitively on sounds and short snatches of words;
- melodising – that is, singing long strands of melody to open vowel sounds.

Rhythmical movement and dancing play

As toddlers gain physical skills their movement vocabulary rapidly expands. So much rhythmical movement is dance-like and music-like that, again, making distinctions becomes difficult. They often repeat actions and movements over and over again to practise and extend. Many rhythmical movements resulted in sound. The daycare had a soft play area with padded mats and cushions.

As the children stomped, bounced, romped and rolled, so the plastic made sounds. During story time they often rolled over, kicked their feet rhythmically on the mat or rubbed, tapped or bounced on the cushions. The activity is multisensory; the kinaesthetic sensations of their own muscular movement, the aural feedback of the sounds the soft-play plastics made and the tactile contact with the surfaces, all merge into one experience.

Music play with instruments and sound-makers

Toddlers continue to apply their developing manipulative skills to making sounds from many sources. The objects may be specifically designed and selected to be a source of interesting sound or things they find. They continue the grip and shake, tap one object on another or on a surface, actions which were characteristic of later babyhood. Very often regular banging or tapping is grouped in short bursts of regular beats followed by a pause. These 'burst–pause' patterns appear to be a characteristic feature of babies' and toddlers' activity across many areas.

Listening

Toddlers, if they are given the opportunity, have the ability to focus listening, to listen to music intently and for quite long periods of time. When they are really listening, with locked-in, wide-eyed attention, fixed gaze and full alertness, they are often quite immobile. This is particularly so if there is somebody performing to watch.

Recorded music played where there is space to move usually produces a physical response. Many parents are familiar with the knees bend, bouncing movement with which toddlers characteristically dance to music. Another common movement is to stretch both arms out to the side and twirl slowly on the spot. This may also be a kind of basic movement pattern which young children apply in dancing to music (Gorali-Turel, 1999).

Many young children spend more time encased in car seats than any previous generation. Music for the car is an important dimension of music listening in many car-owning family lives. In talking with parents about their use of music in the car with children, I found that many involve their children in their choice of tapes, sing along or draw their attention to interesting aspects of the music.

Toddlers are also interested in all kinds of sounds around us – the melodies of mobile phones, the bleep of the microwave, the washing machine – and the ways in which they can be manipulated with buttons and touch controls. This interest can be fostered as part of everyday life experience.

Researchers have found that if children are spending long periods of time in environments where the television is playing continuously, or background music is played, they begin to switch off their listening alertness and to lose some of their ability to perceive acutely. For this reason, carers may want to think carefully about the way they use music and television with their children. Certainly, in the daycare, we found that when the recorded music was playing in the background, even though it was unobtrusive, the children vocalised less in their general play.

General processes

When we look at children's play through the kinds of lenses which music offers, some underpinning processes begin to emerge. What do I mean by this? I have in mind to understand children's play in terms of rhythmical regularities and patterning, to hear the way their voices modulate in pitch and to plot the imaginative transformations which take place as children extend their play with musical ideas. Here I link up with Chapter 2 in which I suggested that children are creating forms of organisation which 'hold on' to things in time and space through rhythmical regularities and expressive shapes.

The simplest form of regularity is to repeat the same thing over and over again – and children do this many times in their play. They repeat a syllable sound, 'doo, doo, doo', and change its pitch, change its pace. Or they create more complex forms of regularity by repeating short patterns or sequences of ideas, or by repeating them and beginning to transform in some kind of anticipatable way.

An example of this is the game of 'Peep-o'. The adult and child play it together, or I have seen toddlers play it alone 'as if' with others. The game extends with variations on the theme – the waiting period is longer, or shorter, the 'Peep-o' louder or softer, the surprise sudden and quick or long-drawn-out and teasing. These are ways of organising small ideas across time, ways of thinking, or getting hold of ideas which are not only fundamental to music, but characterise other forms of meaningful organisation. Most ways of thinking require the organisation of events in time, how they change and develop in sequence over time and being able to anticipate consequences. Most important in all this is that feeling and sensitivity to others, or intersubjectivity as Trevarthen (1980) terms it, is bound up in the process. Playing 'Peep-o' is all about the sharing of feeling; looking or not looking, surprise and delight, points of connection between two people.

Adults have an important role in developing children's ability to organise their ideas in time, to anticipate, to infer what might come next. Song and rhyme games contain simple structures or regularity with variation. Bruner has explained how these structures can support language (Bruner and Sherwood, 1975) and Trevarthen (1995) implies that they have a more fundamental cognitive role. I am suggesting that music, in its broadest sense as the imaginative and expressive organisation of ideas in time, is fundamental to learning to learn.

Adults responding to children's spontaneous music play

Noticing, listening and tuning in to children's spontaneous music play is the first stage – then, importantly, hearing the music in it. John Blacking was an ethnomusicologist who spent much time studying the musical life of the Venda people in South Africa (Byron, 1995). He tells of seeing a small child tap a metal plate at the meal table. We might imagine that in our early childhood settings the child would likely be told to stop, maybe the plate removed. In this Venda family an adult joined in with the child's tapping, creating a rhythmical percussion duet. This small incident is telling because it demonstrates how the child's spontaneous act was heard and interpreted as music, added to and extended by the adult into a small musical event. The music was made between the two playing together, with the adult playing musically on the child's terms. Moreover, this was a commonplace, everyday occasion.

Learning to listen to young children's music and hear it as music may take some practice. In writing about this I suggested that the adults have to suspend their usual ideas of what music sounds like and struggle to enter a children's musical world (Young, 1995). In children's visual arts, adults have become practised at knowing what children's artwork will look like. For music, we lack the long tradition of honouring, collecting and analysing children's own made music so that we have long established understandings of what it will sound like.

In the descriptions which follow I pick out responses and interactions of practitioners to children in a daycare setting. Many of these were almost at the level of intuition, as many of the parent–child interactions would be. They were part of a fabric of playful, supportive, affectionate interaction with the children.

> Kane (seventeen months) sits on a rocker. 'Ee-aw, ee-aw,' he sings quite loudly. Alex is close by and looking over the fence, talking to another worker, but when he hears Kane, he turns and sings 'See, saw, see, saw' back to Kane, at exactly the same pitch, echoing Kane. He then turns back and continues his adult conversation.

> Rachel is sitting on a settee, foot outstretched, and Ellie (fourteen months) half sits on her foot, bouncing herself up and down with a regular knees-bend movement. Rachel improvises a little rhythmical chant-song to accompany her bounces – 'Ella, Ella, Ella, Ella.'

In both these two observations, the adults respond to the children's spontaneous musical behaviours. Kane is reproducing 'See, saw, see, saw' from the well known children's rhyme, and in his singing he is synchronising this with his movements as he rocks. Alex replies with an echo, thus communicating to Kane that his song is heard and recognised. Rachel's moment of connection with Ella is enhanced with the small, improvised singing and movement game which develops from Ella's bouncing movement. Alex responds, Rachel matches, and both extend the child's first contribution by something in kind which they add. It is a simple but powerful means for making connecting points with the child's spontaneous musical behaviours. In general play situations, adults who have long periods of continuity with the children can find these small moments. In joining with them, the adults share positive emotions through the musical communications. They arise from familiarity, from having and sustaining close relationships with the children.

> Jamie (twenty-two months) is playing with a small red plastic bowl which is part of the kitchen set-up in his daycare room. He has it on his head. He stamps along calling 'Ho, ho, ho' in

a loud voice. Sam, one of the carers, is sitting by Jamie on the floor. He proffers her the bowl, upside down. 'Tap, tap, tap,' she says as she simultaneously taps on the bowl. Jamie copies her many times over, saying 'Tap, tap, tap,' in imitation of Sam, and tapping the bowl on the floor. Next he places a small plastic toy inside and bounces it up and down in the plastic bowl, making a noise. He rattles two plastic cups in the bowl in a similar way, watching and listening as they joggle around.

In this short episode, lasting only a couple of minutes, Jamie's play quickly moves through many different changes. It is these quick changes which lead many to describe young children's play as random and exploratory. Yet it is quite clear, when looking closely, how each new idea evolves from the one before. At the same time, it is valuable to tease out those strands of his play which are specific to music learning. These are:

- rhythmic movement – whole-body movement when he stamps and regular tapping with his hands;
- vocalising short patterns – his own 'ho, ho, ho' to match his movement;
- making sounds with objects and exploring the variations in the quality of sound;
- ability to copy short rhythmic vocal and tapping rhythms.

Sam joined in with Jamie's play and offered a new idea of tapping. But notice how Sam's three-beat idea 'Tap, tap, tap' matches Jamie's own 'Ho, ho, ho'. Jamie took up this new version and incorporated it. This incorporation of ideas offered by the adult doesn't always happen, as adults who work with young children all the time so well know – sometimes it does, sometimes not. Perhaps, crucially, Jamie had offered Sam the bowl in the confident expectation that she would play with him in a well matched way.

Children use toys and equipment for their own purposes. The red bowl belongs to a role-play kitchen area, but for Jamie it is a stimulus to movement and vocal play, to tapping rhythms, to making rattly sounds. Equally, a drum might be intended for tapping rhythms, but I've seen children use one as a bowl for a hand-washing game. While adults see things as having distinct uses, children exploit the play potential of equipment in whatever direction suits their current priority. As an interesting aside, adults are often concerned when musical instruments are used for something other than musical activity, even if they are specially designed as robust early learning equipment. Yet other toy equipment is often permitted to be used more fluidly.

Everyday music

By everyday music I mean musical activity which is integrated into the care and play routines in the home, daycare, nursery. The practitioners in the daycare centre I came to know well evolved an environment in which recorded music, song and vocal play featured as part of the everyday routines. Some staff were more outgoing singers than others, but all used song in ways which matched their musical personalities.

Songs were incorporated as part of play, as part of physical and emotional care, as part of the social life between adults and children and to enhance early learning. The songs came from a very wide repertoire of children's songs, popular and traditional, or adult songs. Some were made up on the spur of the moment, mostly one-to-one, unpremeditated, spontaneous. Some were little made-up snatches which the staff had evolved over time. Some were known songs changed to fit certain purposes. Songs were used to help manage moods and emotions; to calm, to enliven, to support, to reassure. Songs were used to be responsive to the children's needs; to make contact, to be noticed, to be comforted, for a moment of fun, of loving.

Songs at sleep time

> To settle the toddlers for a daytime nap in a daycare nursery the practitioners had a wide repertoire of quiet, soothing songs. The children lie on soft giant pillows and their key workers sit by them and gently rub the backs of those who are not yet asleep – two at a time if need be.

Songs as part of care routines

> Ryan (twenty-six months) was settling into daycare and needed his nappy changing. Maureen knows he likes a certain football song. She sings it to entertain him and help dissipate any tension he is experiencing with the nappy changing.

In winter putting on twelve sets of outdoor coats, hats and gloves was time-consuming. A game evolved of 'zip, zip, zipping' up the coats, with upward vocal sounds for 'zipping'. It helped the children to wait patiently while the zips were fastened.

Songs for comfort and reassurance

Jamie (nineteen months) had fallen over and hurt his knee. Rachel scooped him up and held him tightly. 'Shall I sing you a song?' she asked. 'What shall I sing?' 'Baa, baa' was requested and sung for him with a tight cuddle and swaying.

Songs to have fun, create pleasure and closeness

Ellie (twenty-five months) lies on her back on a bench outside, next to Natalie. Natalie sings a latest pop song to her, tickles her tummy. 'Where is Ellie? Oh, there she is. Peep-o!' – sung to a snatch of melody from the pop song.

Songs to encourage, particularly physical effort

Michael (thirteen months) is only recently walking. He is trying to climb on to the small trampoline. Rachel leaves him to struggle independently but sings to him quite vigorously, 'It's raining, it's pouring – there you go, Michael,' as if to encourage him.

Singing and outdoor play

Mei-lin (twenty-four months) and Precious (twenty-six months), in turn, stand at the top of the slide in the outdoor play area. They hold on to both armrests and jump up and down on the top ramp, chanting 'Hop, hop, hop, hop, little bunnies,' and once this phrase has been sung they slide down the slide. At the bottom of the slide the nursery practitioner holds both their hands and bounces them in small jumps. 'Hop, hop, hop, hop, little bunnies,' she chants. Then each runs around to repeat the circuit again. This sequence becomes a game which is repeated many times over.

The nursery practitioner noticed, joined in and extended the singing-moving game initiated by Mei-lin and Precious.

The opportunities to integrate song-singing into general play extend to outdoor play. Adults might initiate outdoor ring games with whichever children choose to join in, as one of a range of outdoor play options. Rachel played 'Ring-a, ring-a roses' with those children who wanted to join her.

Providing a song-rich environment

These children are hearing a lot of unaccompanied, close-range singing by people with whom they feel confident and secure. Singing is part of their everyday life. Ideally adults will sing to young children in a range of contexts, at home, in the car, as part of daily routines, for enjoyment and relaxation, for entertainment. Closeness and relating are communicated and reaffirmed in the singing of songs. In this way children can learn that singing is a natural and enjoyable part of adult life, a life-skill. In some families, some early years settings, some communities and cultures, singing is more freely and comfortably part of the everyday than in others. Toddlers' capacity for absorption and learning is considerable, so this is a phase when they need to be hearing a wide range of songs.

I noticed that staff new to the daycare gradually picked up the usual repertoire of songs by listening to the established staff and learning by direct imitation. In this way the singing-rich environment was handed on. This kind of nursery music culture, and the aural learning methods which are part of it, are commonly the way that repertoire is acquired. A new member of staff with experience of other nurseries may bring new songs from another setting. While effective, the repertoire can become static. If staff, on reflection, feel that this is the case, new repertoire can be learnt from CDs or from training days. An early years music specialist can be invited to work in the setting for a period of time in order to evolve with the staff songs (either newly made or traditional) which fit with their children, their families, their community and the adults who work there. Such a process might include:

• inviting parents to contribute songs from home;
• researching the traditional songs of the local community;
• asking adult staff to remember songs;
• composing new songs to commissions requested by parents, staff and children;

- evolving new songs from the spontaneous contributions of the children;
- making up songs to fit the daily routines of the setting.

One-to-one music games between carer and child

Singing games and spoken rhymes continue from the lullabies and play-songs of babyhood. One-to-one singing games usually involve a combination of movement, song and mini-drama. The physical closeness and movement are an important element in these games. Toddlers enjoy more physical boisterousness than they might have tolerated as babies – energetic joggling, sudden tips and spills, or swings high up and down. Many rhymes include physical contact such as tweaking and tickling. Teasing fun, jokes and surprises are often built into the game.

Repetition is key. The child will ask, 'Again, again.' Varying the repetitions, by changing pace, by slowing down or speeding up, doing things unexpectedly all add to the excitement. Variation within an expected format is teaching the child. As with babies, attuned carers will know when the experience has peaked and winding down is required.

When toddlers experience lots of one-to-one or close, small-group singing, it makes it possible for them to find connecting points and participate fully. Songs from CDs, the television or video are quite complex musically. They are usually performed at a fast pace, with dense textures, many words, and have no flexibility. Adults singing one-to-one provide adaptable versions of songs which can be attuned to the needs of individual children.

Peep-o!

Sing this next song and play peep-o with light chiffon scarves or pieces of sari fabric. Equally, it might be played with other props. One nursery setting had a set of see-through plastic plates and we played peep-o with these.

Where is Ja-son? Wish I knew. Pull the scarf down, Peep-o!

Tickling rhyme

> One for her nose [*tickle noses*],
> One for her toes [*tickles toes*],
> And one for her middle where the pizza goes!
> [*Tickle tummy.*]

Knee-rider

> Bouncy, bouncy up and down,
> Bouncy bouncy off to town.
> Bouncy UP! [*lift up high*]
> And bouncy DOWN [*tip down*],
> Bouncy, bouncy all around! [*Joggle about.*]

Finger play

> Slowly, slowly, very slowly creeps the garden snail,
> Slowly, slowly, very slowly up the garden rail.
> Quickly, quickly, very quickly runs the little mouse,
> Quickly, quickly, very quickly all around the house.

Two fingers creep slowly, then run up the child's arm.

Group singing

Bringing together a group of toddlers and their carers to sing songs together, often as part of a circle time which includes stories, is a mainstay of early years practice. For toddlers, participation in group singing is a quite different experience from one-to-one, or one-to-a-few, singing.

I observed many such sessions in many settings. Much importance and value is placed on bringing the children together, on group participation. On occasion children had to be coerced into remaining in the group and taking part. The singing appeared often to be a means of imposing conformity rather than contributing to quality time together. Louie Suthers (2002) recommends what she calls 'clustering' in which the adult presents herself as 'ready to sing' and the children can come and go as they wish. She calls these sociable music activities to distinguish them from one-to-one or fixed group activity.

The toddlers were gathered together in the day care for a circle time which includes story and singing. During the songs I noted the range of ways in which they participated. One or more:

- watched and listened very intently but showed no obvious signs of participating;
- watched and appeared to mouth some of the words without making any sounds or showed small rhythmic movement responses;
- joined in just some of the actions of a song – the 'roly-poly' movement for example – or tried to clap their hands;
- moved, bounced and wriggled in an enthusiastic way, sometimes out of keeping with the nature of the song;
- joined in a little but always lagging a bit behind;
- contributed to a regularly recurring key phrase – or sound – particularly those with strong phonic features like 'ee-i, ee-i, oh';
- contributed the final word of a phrase – for example in 'Twinkle, twinkle' just the 'star', barely spoken.

The range of participation is characteristic of children of this age – indeed, of older pre-school children too. Very often the children's responses lag behind the adult's presentation of the song. So, for example, the 'star' of 'Twinkle, twinkle' is sung just a moment later. If the adult notices a few children joining in this way, then giving time for them to make their contribution with generous pauses is important. The words 'star' and 'are' are not just dominant verbally, but also musically dominant in the rhythmic and melodic structure of the song. Just as the baby anticipates the phrasing structure of the song, so young children can anticipate and begin to make more of a contribution at key moments.

Some of the youngest and newest children in the group deliberately positioned themselves where they could get the best view of the other children. In this way they could watch in order to imitate. They often needed to watch many times before they ventured any kind of active participation. Children who appear outwardly passive but are very involved in listening and watching are quite different from children who are passive because they are overwhelmed or anxious.

Providing an environment for play with sound-makers

Small children's attention is held by beautiful-sounding objects and they will listen with great concentration. Chinese massage bells, brass bells from India, pieces of tinkling chain, tiny, brittle-sounding music boxes, gourds and seed pods, rattles of nut husks are among the things we gathered together just for listening. We brought them out of pockets, small bags and boxes and listened to them with individual children or small groups; sounding, listening, talking and putting away again. Like some special books to look at, there were certain restrictions on when and how the children could get them out.

The next series of short observations will illustrate one approach to providing play for instruments which evolved as part of the project. They are taken from a parent and toddler group which meets weekly in a church hall. The group have assembled a wide range of percussion instruments and were exploring different ways of using them within their setting. They found that one of the most effective ways was to set them out on a table. The hall is not equipped with child-size furniture; the table and chairs were adult size. The table is covered with a cloth to prevent the clatter of instruments on its plastic surface. Parents, all mothers in this group, visit the table with their children, mostly sitting them on their knee, to play together with the instruments.

> One mother, Carole, sits, face-to-face, opposite her daughter Ellie-Louise (two years six months). 'What are you going to use?'
> Ellie reaches for some egg shakers.
> 'All of them? Can you shake them together?'
> Ellie takes bells as well.
> 'Can you make a big noise? Go on, then, shake them. Mummy likes that one. Oooh.'
> Carole has her own instrument and plays with her daughter. 'Ye-ea-ah,' she cheers. 'Ding-a-ling-a-ling! Jingle bells.'
> At this Ellie starts to sing what is just recognisable as 'Jingle bells', and her mother joins in with her singing. Ellie proffers a bell to her mother to play along too.

In this short play episode, mother and child 'give and take' very successfully. Ellie reaches and takes the instruments herself and

Carole is positive and encouraging, particularly in saying she likes the instrument and in her vocalised responses, 'oohs' and 'yeah!' Carole introduced the 'Ding-a-ling', jingle bells idea, which is picked up by Ellie. In turn, she gives her mother back a set of bells to join in. The mother plays with her child, adding to the child's own play by contributing ideas which are well matched. She enhances and extends her daughter's play without being over-directive or controlling.

In another observation, the mother of Jasmine (nineteen months) took a responsive role, allowing the child to take the lead, putting things within reach, modelling playing actions but all the time watching, listening, smiling and commenting, 'Well done,' when her child looked to her for a response. The child was framed by this attentiveness and knew it, secure that the adult would provide just what she needed at the right moment. This adult did not join in by playing musically and freely with Jasmine, but was success-fully supporting her exploration.

In a third observation, the mother is more directing. Her daughter (twenty-three months) plays with one instrument, and reaches for a second, a triangle. The mother says, 'No, you've got to put it down. Play it with a stick.' 'Shall we ring, ting-a-ling? Shall we ring it?' Her child plays a little with the triangle. Now her mother reaches for a bell and hands it. 'Can you do that?' The child takes the bell and drops it on the floor. Perhaps as a result of the mother's more instructive role, play is less fluent.

The greatest need of the child may be for pleasure, approval and encouragement of the sound-making activity. Direct instruction, with a sense of one 'right way' to play the instruments, may close down the child's inclination. But the music play with instruments does need to be provided in such a way that the adults can feel comfortable with it. Excessive noise or very boisterous play with instruments can be unsettling. By setting out the instruments on the table they were out of reach unless the children were brought to play by their mothers one by one. In this way there was no mixed cacophony of free play by a large number children at once: they could listen and receive attentive support. The mothers, in turn, felt reassured that the instruments were handled safely.

The first mother drew the child's attention to the sounds that are made, by 'ding-a-linging' in imitation. Focused listening is funda-mental to music. It is valuable if adults can draw attention to the act of listening and the sound quality itself. There may then be small adjustments which can be modelled or suggested to improve the quality of the sound which is made. For example, hands holding on to a triangle may prevent it from ringing, or a drum set down on the table may be less resonant than when it is held up.

In terms of being physically able to handle and play instruments, the basic sound-making movements of babyhood, shaking and tapping, will continue. Few will continue to need to explore by mouthing. Toddlers can begin to hold and strike one thing on another. It may be beaters or sticks to strike on a stand-alone or gripped instrument, or one instrument striking on to another. The combined effects of, say, a set of bells tapping on to a standing drum can result in an interesting mix of sounds.

The action of holding in one hand and tapping with the other may elude them still. Stands which hold a small assortment of untuned percussion instruments present toddlers with a varied set-up. They helpfully keep instruments in one place on the table and provide a variety of sounds without the difficulty of having to hold and play. More complex playing movements such as scraping a guiro or tipping an ocean drum may need to be modelled. There are many occasions in play with objects which are not designed with music in mind when children will manipulate and listen, tap, shake, put things inside others and rattle, crunch and swish. Alert adults will notice these moments and capitalise on them, perhaps even collecting up interesting sound-making objects. In the daycare, the basket of small metal things was a treasure trove of tinkling, chinking sounds.

While most instruments designed for early years use will survive child handling, taut drum skins, gourd maracas, light wood rattles may be examples of instruments that are pleasing in sound but fragile. There is often a balance to be struck between quality of sound, robustness and expense. The range of sounds offered by 'small hands' percussion often recommended for early years can be quite limited. Opportunities to play plucked sounds – to explore guitar together, for example – to explore deep, resonant sounds, a trip to hear the local church organ, to experience brilliant, loud sounds, to try out a cymbal brought in by secondary school players, will extend their aural experiences. And inviting instrumentalists to come and play for children extends the range even more, although this is likely to be listening only without hands-on. Small children are fascinated by the source of sound and do need to peer up the clarinet bell or tweak the silver keys.

Toddlers will also show different emotional responses to sounds made. Some young children may be stimulated to the point of over-excitement by certain sounds, others may be overwhelmed by shrill, sharp, loud noises and look away. Placing their hands over their ears begins to be a common response when sounds are too much.

Finally

This chapter has described how music with toddlers expands into new worlds as they begin to talk and walk. Yet the theme of the book continues: music as part of play and adults being responsively and creatively playful with music. Babies and toddlers often come together with their carers to take part in group musical activity. This next chapter goes on to consider music play among groups of adult carers and their babies and toddlers.

Chapter 6

Group music play

This chapter will look at:

- general issues
- semi-guided music play sessions
- working with carers
- reviewing and planning
- practicalities

It is common for groups of babies or toddlers and their adult carers to come together for guided or collaborative music play sessions. An important aim in the approach to group work being described here is to encourage and support playful musical engagement between carer and child. Within such a group, the network of relationships weaves complicatedly: carer to child, children to children, carers to carers, group leader (if this is the structure of the group) to children, to adults and to pairs. The criss-crossing of interpersonal dimensions complicates the processes of engaging and interacting through music, words and non-verbal means. Versions of practice from music therapy emphasise sensitivity to forms of relating through music and can be most useful to early years music practice. The emphasis in the approach described in this chapter is on not working to a rigidly planned structure but initiating, following, improvising to allow the group sessions to evolve around the needs of those involved.

The flexible, unpredictable nature of working with the unit-pair of baby or toddler and carer may be quite a different experience for many. Models of workshop, group-work, facilitated or led sessions which work well in other community contexts may not transfer well. Time for reflection about the ways of working with adults, be they parents, childminders, daycare workers or nursery practitioners, and being clear on aims and intentions of the work become important in the process of developing work in this area. Ideally, the process of reflection is supported and built into regular supervisory or review sessions with a colleague.

Toddlers had moved into the central carpet area where a range of small cymbals with large-grip wooden knobs were set out. The practitioner took a pair of cymbals, vocalising 'Bang – !' with a light, high-pitched voice which mimicked the resonance and ring of the small cymbals. Simultaneously she swung both cymbals out in a wide arc. Carers helped the toddlers to take up the cymbals and copy the movement – 'Bang!' They played with the cymbals too or showed surprise and delight as toddlers played with them.

One boy disappeared behind his mother away into a corner of the room, another child preferred to stay on her father's lap and watch. A free-play session developed. The practitioner watched the adults and toddlers and sometimes joined in too, sometimes took up an idea, sometimes not. Then the cymbals were gathered up and put back into a drawstring fabric bag.

Having initiated an idea with the cymbals in a very light-touch way by setting out the equipment and modelling a way of playing, the practitioner withdrew to allow toddlers and parents to develop their play with the cymbals. She took up their cues and joined in with playing sometimes, drawing the session to a close when she sensed it had run its course. Her role was as the child's secondary, not primary, educator.

General issues

Sessions which include music for a group of carers and their babies/toddlers may take many forms.

*   A co-operative activity among a group of carers who gather to make music together with their babies and toddlers – *in a daycare, parent and toddler group.*
*   Sessions led by a leader who decides the content and structure – *music sessions as part of a larger early years organisation, or privately run music groups.*

- Activities guided by pre-written, taped or video activities where the materials have largely been planned beyond the leader and the group – *some franchise music groups, one-off performance arts groups.*
- Semi-structured sessions with a broad purpose which include music – *groups which focus on parenting skills, or supporting language development in the first years.*

Other caregivers – grandparent, childminder, key worker – might be in addition to the parent enlarging the unit, or in place of the parent. Some carers or parents with multiple or very close births may have two or three babies or toddlers in their care.

Aims and purposes

Music sessions for a group of carers and babies or toddlers may be set up to serve a range of purposes and aims, many of which will combine and overlap. In addition, who initiates the sessions and decides the intentions, and how the roles, expectations are negotiated can all be crucial to the forms of participation which develop and to successful outcomes. All participating adults need to be clear about the aims and purposes, and ideally have a sense of ownership. When all have been involved from the outset, and in ongoing review, they are more likely to want to commit and continue. More likely, too, that the group work will be adapted to the needs of the group and be culturally and socially sensitive. The aims may include:

- to encourage music-making (particularly song singing) between carers and children, both in the session and beyond at home and in the community;
- to raise awareness of how very young children develop in music and the carer's role in that development;
- to provide first steps in music learning;
- to encourage broader skills such as carer and child playing together, language development;
- to support parenting skills;
- to provide a communal occasion.

Broad aims such as those which typically appear in documentation for projects and policies are likely to need more detailed thinking through before they can be turned into practice. Local needs and priorities will determine aspects of the work. It might be useful to consider to what extent the sessions will:

* model activities – *for carers to take away and do in their setting, at home*;
* encourage participation – *for quality experiences during the session*;
* inform – *provide information, e.g. about young children's musical development, of music learning processes*;
* train music skills – *teach parents and/or their children certain music skills*;
* use music as a medium to support other skills – *support certain skills through music, such as interaction or language development*;
* provide ideas – *suggest music-play activities, resources*;
* provide materials – *give song sacks, cassettes*.

and to be clear on whether experiences are intended mainly for the adults, or for the child and adult together, or primarily the child?

Differentiating

In addition to group needs, identifying the individually differing needs of children and their carers and ensuring they are met is an additional challenge within any group.

Carers may well have varying reasons for setting up or attending the session, and those who initiate the group will be alert to these different motivations. For example, many 'drop-ins' are a meeting place for the carers where they can socialise while their children play together, making use of the nursery or playgroup facilities. In such settings, the parents, childminders, may be reluctant to give up what is an important and necessary time out from the children to take part in music activities. In other settings adults may come to the sessions with fears about exposure to the group as a whole, both in music and in parenting terms. It can be easy for those fired with enthusiasm and ideals for music work to ride roughshod over some of these aspects which influence participation.

Ensuring the work is broadly inclusive of all parents and all children will cover a range of considerations. These may be practical adaptations, equipment or resources for children and carers with special needs. Catering for parents and children who do not have English as their first language may require translators and adaptation of the session content. Being respectful of different cultural traditions can be assured if all participants are involved in planning. Ensuring access to parents of different social class can bring to light different expectations for their children and styles of parenting. All these issues may challenge assumptions which underlie approaches to working held by some of those involved and require rethinking.

Semi-guided music play sessions

Here is a description of a session for parents and babies aged between six and eighteen months, led by a trained early years music specialist who is also a professional jazz singer. What is significant about this session is the degree of involvement of the child–adult pairs so that several times during the session the activities are handed back to the children and parents to continue and sustain. The leader, having initiated activities, often becomes redundant. Within the structure of the session there is freedom for parents and children to participate in their own way, to play together. The session activities may be planned and introduced by the leader, but the session has more the feel of a guided musical play session for parents and children.

> The parents and babies gather – the youngest is around six months, the eldest is eighteen months. The session gradually begins as the lead adult quietly sings a regular 'hello' song, very quietly and gently. One child stands close to her, watching intently. One parent sings the hello song to her child quite independently, in her own way. The leader then sings hello to each child in turn, moving on her knees a little closer around the carpet, making eye contact if it is reciprocated by the child. One hides her eyes, another stands boldly in front of her, one sits in the crook of her parent's knee and looks.
> The lead adult addresses the parents, asking them if they will feel able to join in the animal noises of the next activity – sharing a joke and encouraging them to play. She has an animal picture book. With the chicken she sings in jazz style, a free 'cock-a-doodle-doo' song. The parents join in with vocal and movements in imitation of the animals. Most of the children

listen and watch. The activity is linked with a simple animal song. Next comes the cow – freely vocalised again, then the cat. The parents 'miaow' to their children. One child sits firmly on her parent's knee, being cuddled. The parent appears uncomfortable with the activity and so the adult leader, 'miaows' to her child on her behalf.

The leader moves to the side of the room and produces something under a little cloth. 'What have I got here?' she asks, full of anticipation. Under the cloth are enough small children's rattles for children and adults all to have one. Everyone rattles to accompany her singing of a rattle song. The song extends into tapping rattles on parts of the body. The parents model for their children, who participate in varying ways. The adults play freely for a moment with their children and the rattles. The lead adult simply watches and remains quiet. Then she begins the 'putting away song' – the 'Farmer's in his den' tune is used with made-up words every time something must be returned and put away.

The adult leader takes up her life-size 'baby' doll and borrows one of the children's shoes. She begins a song-rhyme – 'Do I put the shoe on my ear, on my nose, on my hand?' – slowly spoken in a rhythmical chant. The children watch and listen. One toddling child comes up and pushes the shoe in her hand on to the doll's foot. She repeats the rhyme many times, with variations of dynamic, pace and intonation.

The adult reaches across to a portable CD player and puts on music for moving rhythmically around the room. The adults pick up their children and dance with them, twizzling around. The leader joins in and playfully visits adult and child pairs in turn. The next CD is for resting and playing with some bubbles. A pot for each parent to blow to match the mood and quality of the music. The same putting-away song signals the returning of the bubble tubs.

A goodbye song brings the session to a close – goodbye to each child in turn.

In this next list the main features of the session are picked out:

• A regular routine with songs which begin and end. This predictability is reassuring to both children and adults, who can come to know what to expect. It also enables the parents to participate more fully, as with the parent who started the hello song independently with her child. The routine provides a transition into and out of the group session.

* During the session the leader allowed the parents ample time to interact with their children. She often initiated activities and then stood back to allow the parents to continue, watching carefully to see if her input or support could assist the process, as with the parent who felt uncomfortable with the animal noises activity. To make themselves productively redundant in this way may feel odd to leaders who are used to performing and actively leading the session.

* The session leader spoke very little, except occasionally to address the parents.

* The activities flowed easily one into another, belying the careful planning and the careful watching of participation during the session which underpinned this.

* There was a variety of activity – listening, movement, singing, rhyming, language play, instrumental play, visualisation – packed into one short session. The leader plans her sessions against a checklist to ensure a range of activity.

* The session contained a wide variety of music: two different qualities of recorded music, several songs of different styles, pace and melodic character, rhythmic rhyming, improvised vocal and instrumental play and the varied sounds of the rattles.

There is a distinction to be drawn between the adult carers learning to sing a song as a performance and singing the song to the children they care for. The song is, essentially, a vehicle for adult–child relating. The emphasis is on the qualities of musical interaction, affective communication through music, rather than musical performance. Drawing attention to the way children are participating helps to emphasise this distinction. Knowing that they are singing the song for the child takes away what for some can be an unnerving sense of being listened to as singers by other adults. On another level, some tentative parents, very young mothers, depressed or anxious parents may find it easier if the focus is on their baby or toddler and interactions are directed to and through their children.

The songs were often personalised by addressing the children by name, making some reference to what they were wearing, or the colour of their hair. Alternatively the songs were contextualised by relating them to a story-book, to actions, a game, the rattles and bubbles. The leader improvised words and actions within the songs and didn't always sing the songs in their entirety, repeating key snatches or single phrases of a song to match an action or sound of animals or rattles. Songs were also used to carry the session along – to start it, to conclude, to signal putting things away. The carers were actively engaging their children through modelling, showing, encouraging, praising and playing with them. The range of types and forms of involvement enabled in this session could also be identified in the adult–toddler play at the music instrument table described in the previous chapter. Music group work can be conceived, therefore as a kind of music activity resource which provides forms of active participation and engagement between adult and child. This idea of involvement needs to be distinguished from the arousal which can be generated by an adult leader in entertainer mode. A strong entertainer-leader often leaves the adults somewhat confused about their role in relation to their children, and the session offers little hand-over. A model of active performer/passive audience characterises many performance traditions in Western musical culture but it does not translate well into early years practice.

The effectiveness of the session hinged on expressive features of the leader's interaction with the group. It is a form of interaction which is both musical and interpersonal; the two overlap, each sensitising the other. She used her speaking voice sparingly, quite quietly and at a slow pace. She did not adopt a child-directed style unless directly addressing the children – as in 'What have I got here?' when introducing the rattles – when she adopted the characteristic exaggerated inflection in her voice. The songs were presented very fluidly, as an improvisation, with pauses to look at children, to fit in improvised words or spoken asides. At the same time her body-language style was relaxed and quiet, with no sudden gestures or over-paced movements. As she worked with the group she was very alert to her social space in relation to the children and adults. If coming close to the children, she looked for cues from the child that it is welcome, or not. At the same time, she moved to different positions in the room so that there was variety, but no parents were left on the margins of the group.

The leader's musical skills, as a professional jazz singer, enriched the session. The story-based animal sounds were wonderfully improvised in jazz style. But she did not overwhelm the

session. The priority remained, not a display of her skills nor entertainment, but an enabling of the participation of the group. The
Dutch training she had received to be an early years music leader
is intensive and focuses on group-work skills, children's development in music, repertoire and activities (van Gestel, 2002).
Here is a version of the shoe song she used in the session.

Here's my shoe!   Here's my shoe!   Where do I put it?   Wish I knew!

Then she asked, 'Do I put it on my ear? Do I put it on my nose?
Do I put it on my hand?' and other or more parts of the body, and
then, finally, 'No, I put it on my foot!' The song can be continued
to other pieces of clothing – a glove, a hat.

Working with carers

Respect for the parents' and other carers' prior knowledge and
experience is essential, together with awareness of how professionalism, particularly music professionalism, can be disempow-
ering. The active involvement in the musical activity of group
sessions by the adults who are significant to the child is essential.
It passes on to the child a positive disposition towards taking part
in music. If the adult appears reluctant, the child will immediately
pick this up. In carer and baby music groups which are collabora-
tively run, such as in a mother-and-toddler group, it is likely that
all will contribute songs they know to a shared repertoire. While
levels of adult involvement in these session may vary, it is taken
as a given that all participate.

However, playful musical involvement, particularly in group
sessions, may come more easily to some carers than to others. The
session can feel like a public display of their parenting, child-
minding, caring skills which some may find daunting. For some
adults, learning to play with the children in their care may be difficult. They may be more comfortable with the physical care and
nurturing aspects of the parenting role but find it difficult to respond
to their children's need for play. For other adults the music may
present the areas of difficulty. On the positive side, parents are

highly motivated to do whatever they can for the good of their children, and this motivation will often override other concerns. The sessions can also enable carers to rediscover the pleasure and value of musical experiences with their child. Their needs – musical, social, emotional – and need for fun and pleasure are provided for as much as the child's.

To facilitate the group music processes, co-operating adults or session leaders will need to observe child behaviour, adult behaviour and the two operating in an interdependent relationship. This is particularly challenging. The interactions in a music session between adult and child will be primarily non-verbal and spontaneous. The music session may bring knots of difficulty within the adult–child relationship to the surface.

> The mother of Hannah (thirteen months) had attended the class irregularly because, she said her child 'did not like the class', was shy and nervous of the other children. This mother sat apart from the rest of the circle and held Hannah close to her on her lap. The practitioner felt that it was the mother who was the shy and nervous one. Her actions and comments were focused on reassuring her and helping her to feel part of the group. As the mother relaxed over the course of a few sessions, so she felt able to release Hannah to participate more fully.

> Both parents of Ben (eighteen months) attend the group. He is a robust, confident child who has no inhibitions in going straight up to the practitioner to snatch what she is showing, or then running boisterously and noisily around the outside of the circle, irrespective of the activity. The practitioner feels that the parents are proud of their energetic, outgoing child and enjoy seeing him 'perform'. While not wishing to diminish their enjoyment of their son, she feels they should be more alert to the group as a whole. She is also interested that they often look and smile at his actions to one another but leave Ben to act independently. She suggests that the parents take turns in working with their son in a partnership and that the other parent might enjoy observing.

In these two examples the group facilitator observes the interaction between carer (parents in these two instances) and child and sees that the child's behaviour in the group can be related directly to the nature of that relationship. Protective behaviours and letting go, all from the secure base of the floor-sitting carer, are often played out in music group sessions. Of course, disposition, personality and other characteristics also affect the child's participation. But the carer is subtly encouraging or discouraging the child to explore by body-language cues. The carer may have needs and difficulties which will be articulated through the relationship to affect the child. The practitioner, by alert observations and reflecting on these, makes small adjustments to how she enables both carers and children to participate in the session. She redirects, subtly, through the activities themselves, directing small comments about participation to the children, yet by this process sending messages back to the carers.

There will be issues, just below the surface, in any group session, as to how much carers should control and direct the children to participate in the session and how much, for example, the children can be allowed to roam freely. As can be seen from the observations, carers will vary – one allowing the child to behave very freely, another hugging the child on her lap. Underlying these caring styles will be styles of attachment, carers who are perhaps struggling to bond or over-protective. It may also be that some caring and participatory styles may conflict with the session leader's conception and plans for how the session might proceed.

The usual group gathering in a circle does encourage participation but adults can come to depend on a leader too much. Leaders who move fluidly around, or even move away from the circle to its outer margins, may encourage more independent participation. If the practitioner presents a very formal model of participation, the adult may feel under duress to make their baby or toddler 'conform and perform'. Being able to easily observe other children across the circle can also lead carers to compare their own and their child's participation in the group with that of others. This can be another source of pressure to coerce their children into taking part in ways which are not suited to either of them. Carers, anxious for their children to participate, may need the reassurance that to 'just listen' – or even sleep through the session – is fine. There may be other times and other groups when the opportunity to compare may be helpful. One music practitioner (Oldfield and Bunce, 2001, p. 31) tells of a teenage parent who was able to relax with her baby in music-making because he was so responsive in a group session and to feel competent in her parenting skills.

Two experienced music practitioners explored other ways of forming the group, informally clustering and changing the formations during the session to overcome some of the disadvantages of the circle formation. They included in their sessions music and movement activities in which everyone is simultaneously active and moving around the room. This diversion focused attention between adult to child. They also set up semi-structured activities where simultaneous participation was not expected – 'All just try this one out in your own time and own way' – thus allowing for different experiences and expressions of a similar activity.

All this discussion leads to the overall comment – easy to say but difficult to achieve in practice – that there needs to be plenty of flexibility in group music work with babies and toddlers for every kind of engagement, from being fast asleep to screaming rejection. Group leaders may need to encourage certain kinds of behaviour on the part of the adults. The following offers a set of guidelines for participating carers:

- positive and enjoyable participation with their child, rather than a directive style;
- acceptance of a child's choice not to participate – perhaps to toddle off or watch passively;
- pleasure and interest in extrovert participation on the part of some children without overemphasising it, such as praising or clapping;
- not comparing the children's participation;
- appropriate interventions to encourage participation from a child – primarily modelling, moving or singing along with.
  (Based on Guilmartin and Levinowitz, 1994)

Communicating and sharing

Ideally there will be continuity between the session and the everyday home lives of group members. The extent and nature of the continuity will be determined also by the type of group and by its aims and purposes. Approaches to continuity will include:

- encouraging parents to bring information, observations, video recordings of their children's musical activities at home;
- encouraging parents to contribute their own songs, recordings, games and those of their family, community;

- encouraging parents to bring cassettes/CDs which their children have particularly liked;
- offering a 'song satchel' – a cassette of songs the children sing, plus words and pictures to go home with different parents each week;
- providing dictaphones – to record songs in the session as an *aide-mémoire* and for parents to bring back recordings of music-making by their children at home;
- setting up a lending library for parents of songbooks with CDs included;
- providing written materials, resource books with ideas and information;
- keeping record cards for each child to which parents can also contribute. Add notes at the end of a session in discussion with parents;
- scheduling a general 'free time', loosely structured for talking together, looking at video recordings from the session and observing children's participation, looking at songbooks, puppets, instruments etc.;
- making specific reference to continuing activities at home.

It may be valuable with some groups to hold a session for the adults only.

Carer-only sessions

These sessions may include:

- reflections upon carers' own backgrounds, experiences of music and attitudes towards music;
- discussions about the musical life of their locality, community;
- how they would wish the musical experiences of their children to be different;
- explanations of the content of the music sessions, descriptions of activities and the purposes behind their choice;
- some practice of songs and activities from the sessions;
- explanations of activities which could be carried out at home.

Reviewing and planning

Most of a session facilitator's work, much more than is usually accounted for, will be carried out beyond the specific music session: keeping notes and reflecting on the progress of sessions so far, researching materials and information, thinking up new ways of working, finding equipment, organising and managing it, planning the sessions and writing evaluations.

An informal, co-operative song-sharing session may seem to need little planning, except prior thinking of some songs to feed into the session if it flounders. And preparation of some recording system if some parents are afraid they will forget any new songs. But even these sessions would benefit from reflective discussion about the children's responses and participation, new materials, games and activity ideas.

Following

Allowing adults and children to take an active role in determining how the session will develop needs careful consideration. The following list includes a range of approaches for setting up semi-structured music sessions:

* Assemble a bag of puppets or soft toys, and what the group do is led by what the babies pull out of a bag.
* Set up playmats with Duplo people for shared singing play.
* Play live or recorded music for free or modelled dancing activities.
* Provide a range or selected instruments or a gathering drum for a play-together session.
* Have a 'song share' where parents introduce lullabies and play-songs they sing to their babies and toddlers or remember from their own childhoods.
* Provide parachutes, streamers, lengths of cloth, to stimulate swinging, swaying and other playful movement and vocal activities.
* Ask parents to bring recorded music to play for quiet moments.

Modelling

Every facet of the leader/facilitator's behaviour will be providing an implicit model. In this way, the lead adult can redirect aspects of behaviour, for example by handling the instruments in a particular way or drawing attention to aspects of children's participation. Explicit modelling may include:

- how to handle, to play instruments;
- attentive listening;
- ways of singing and dancing appropriate to young children;
- ways of holding, interacting with and moving with babies and toddlers by using parenting dolls or a large soft toy;
- being musically playful and spontaneous;
- being observant of young children's interpersonal and musical cues.

Leading

Start-ups and endings

Starting and ending the session in the same, almost ritualistic, ways provides predictability. The children and adults can come to associate certain songs and certain actions and events with the start and conclusion. Groups will vary and there may be a point at which a starting or concluding song becomes tired, and a new one provides a much-needed moment of variety.

Some kind of winding down to end the session in a quiet, relaxing mode:

- a sung lullaby with cuddling and rocking, soft toys to help;
- lullaby played on an instrument to watch and listen;
- quiet recorded music to lie on the floor together;
- baby lying on floor in front of parent, gentle massage movements with a song;
- pieces of fabric to waft to a song, to coddle baby in;
- very quiet sounds, tinkling from a mobile, to watch and listen.

Routines and repetitions

Repetition from session to session and a set routine within sessions are important. Ideally, the children will give the sense that enough is enough. The kinds of activities are kept very stable and only one or two variations or new introductions are made in each session. Children enjoy engaging with what becomes familiar and routinised and appear to need such repetition. Simple checklists can ensure breadth within routine:

- one listening activity;
- one movement activity or singing game;
- one activity with sound-makers;
- one or two puppet, toy or other prop songs;
- songs which involve musical contrasts, such as loud/quiet, slow/fast in many variations.

They can also ensure a range of one-to-one activities between adult and child:

- toy-focused singing games;
- instrument-focused activities;
- story-book or picture-focused singing games;
- lap bouncing and singing games;
- carrying and swinging movement games;
- holding-hands movement games.

Aural variety is very important. A session which is just sung may sound very 'samey' to the child. Recorded music and instrumental sounds introduce variety.

Pacing

Pacing of the sessions is important with higher-energy, stimulating activities followed by lower-pace, quieter activities. Whole-body dancing movements to recorded music, an energetic song, followed by something more static and aural. The adult leader will initiate the changes of pace, reading the group cues. Adults working with babies need to be very aware of not alarming them with overload, overactive or overly intrusive activities, particularly in early sessions.

Positioning

Planning for varieties of grouping, positioning facilitates the participation and independence of adults and children. Will the group facilitator remain in one position looking out at the group, circulate around the outside and visit each pair in turn, move around to different positions in the room? Do the babies or toddlers want to face the parent or face out? This may vary with different personalities or with different ages. And within these positionings always leaving options and not dictating that a song or an activity must be done a certain way.

Practicalities

The quality of the accommodation is an important issue. Places and spaces for music may be too small or too large, noisy or poorly furnished. Music practitioners who visit settings to work in music are often frustrated by these basics. Those employing music practitioners need to be aware of just how the accommodation and group size can influence the effectiveness of what can be achieved. Having read several evaluation reports from music project work, it is clear just how crucial these details can be to success of the work. Small groups of adults and carers, never more than eight or ten, are ideal, and just five may be the most comfortable and effective group size.

As far as is ever possible, all those involved should be insisting on well lit, warm, clean, comfortable and aesthetically pleasing spaces in which to work. Early childhood groups are accommodated in all kinds of buildings, many of which serve multiple purposes. Few have quality studio or workshop spaces with suitable flooring, sympathetic acoustics, natural light and pleasing decor. Equally, where early childhood groups meet there is a tendency, in the UK certainly, to clutter the spaces with play equipment, tables, chairs and so on. Open spaces enable different kinds of things to happen.

Many carers will have more than one pre-school child. Sessions may be intended for one age phase or provide a crèche or an assistant who can occupy siblings. Alternatively classes may accept all children within broad age bands and provide broadly based activities with different modes of participation expected from children of varying ages. However, such are the differences between a six-month-old and a nearly four-year-old that keeping groups, as far as is possible, to age bands makes practical sense.

Ideally, another 'helper' to the session is a great bonus. This helper can double with language skills, can help with the practicalities of baby arrivals and departures, such as buggy parking, unwrapping baby from outdoor clothing, and can ease in the latecomer. In addition groups will want to establish some simple conventions of participation established by the group which will also ensure health and safety.

The active space is usually defined by a circular rug, a piece of carpet, a blanket or a soft play mat. In large spaces this helps to gather the toddlers in. For those working in non-purpose-built spaces, it assures a safe, clean floor surface, particularly for crawlers, and somewhere comfortable enough for parents to sit. Shoes-off on the rug for adults and children can be a practical way to facilitate movement. Bare feet and soft floor surfaces also encourage gentle, quiet movement.

Any equipment should be plentiful, ideally one each for child and adult, so that all can join in playing. Real and beautiful instruments, sound-makers and play things convey messages of value and respect. It can be easy for frequently used equipment to become tired. Books and other visuals need to be large enough for all to see, ideally the 'big book' kind now produced for group story activities. Puppets, soft toys and other props provide a valuable stimulus, but toddlers may crowd. Either be ready for the crowding or set some ground rules.

Finally

From group work with babies and toddlers, and their carers, we move on to consider the next age phase, growing up to be three years old and then on to four. During this age phase young children begin to become more independent of their one-to-one or one-to-a-few carers.

Chapter 7

On to three and then four

(I) Voice-play and singing

This chapter will look at:

- spontaneous voice-play
- adults: joining in with voice-play
- creating an environment for singing play
- learning to sing songs

Growing up to be three years old and then on to four, the young child becomes increasingly more independent and competent. This pre-school phase spans roughly the period from toddlerhood to the age at which children enter full-time schooling some time in their fourth year. During this age phase most children in the UK are beginning to attend some form of pre-school. They move gradually into settings of playgroups, nurseries and pre-schools from home or from other forms of daycare setting. With this transition they arrive in more educationally structured environments. Here adult to children ratios increase so that it is less likely, unless they have special needs, that children will have adults who are allocated specifically to their care.

All pre-school settings, even the most formally organised, make spaces and equipment available for children to play spontaneously. In the free-play times young children continue to integrate musical play as one strand of their ongoing activity, singing to themselves as they play with the trains or making rhythmic movement patterns as they thump dough. But unlike their self-initiated activity in other domains, such as painting, model-making, role play, this musical activity goes largely unnoticed. Play with instruments may be provided for, but otherwise what the adults count as music, and what is usually planned for in music, is confined to a group circle time, when children gather for an adult-led song and rhyme session. These may be particularly important years for fostering a positive disposition as an active music-maker: to sing, to play instruments and move. If spontaneous efforts and activity are largely ignored, or at worst closed down because they are 'noisy' or 'boys don't sing', then the effects drive deep into the sense of self as musical. Once absorbed, negative dispositions are very resilient. Ours is a culture which is not good at fostering positive identities of ourselves as musical people. Setting about redressing some imbalances cannot start too early.

The strong message of this book which I hope is emerging as the chapters unfold is music as play: children's musicality as one important strand of play, one which underpins many other aspects of development, children playing with music and adults recognising, understanding, providing for and partnering children's music play. This chapter continues with these themes and focuses on vocal play. It begins with children's spontaneous vocal play and then moves gradually towards more formal kinds of activity to cover children learning songs. Again, unlike art educators, who can print a small sample of children's drawing, in order to capture the reality of children's vocal play, I have to write short descriptions. As you read, allow your knowledge of children and imagination to bring them to life.

Spontaneous voice-play

I found that children around three years old are the most prolific producers of spontaneous vocal play in nursery settings in comparison with younger children or those closer to four who are well used to nursery. These older 'pre-schoolers' played together more and so talked more to one another, thus diminishing the amount of singing. If this is the case, then around three may represent a 'window of opportunity' for the designing of interventions which connect with and build on children's spontaneous vocalisations. On the occasions when I did collect spontaneous singing and vocalising from the older children, it often showed more sophisticated features, evidence that children's own singing continues to develop. But as educational settings become more formal, they can sing less freely and so this stream of activity goes underground, to re-surface in play out of school, in the playground with others or at home alone.

It is impossible to draw a dividing line between speech and singing with young children, for they vocalise with words, melodise, intone, chant, whoop and whizz their voices as a continuous sound track to their play. It is richly imaginative and expressive, texturising all they do. It intertwines language and music and blends with movement, play with objects and sociable play with others. In the second chapter I suggested that music with underfours was largely about preventing capacities from disappearing. One of the reasons vocalising goes unheard is that we have tended to focus on the visible, physical and object-based outcomes of play, and the rational, verbal communicating, rather than on the holistic nature of the play process itself.

What follows are descriptions of Ryan (three years two months) taken from a continuous free-play period lasting an hour and five minutes. They are mini-descriptions, selected to illustrate different types of spontaneous singing. Along with descriptions of his singing I have given details of his play. Ryan attends this nursery most days. Being familiar with the adults and surroundings enables him to settle confidently and contentedly into self-initiated and sustained free-flow play. He was one of the children who vocalised almost continuously as he played, so he was not typical of the majority of children. These snapshots of Ryan's sing-play will provide a guide for looking and listening to other young children in other settings.

For a short period before the free-play hour, the children gathered for a formal, adult-led singing session. This began with the regular opening song 'Hello Everyone!' and continued with a collection of songs for winter and Christmas and some usual nursery favourites. It is interesting, given how prolifically he sings in his free play, that Ryan did not appear to take any particular interest in these songs nor make any attempt to join in.

Free-flow singing

> Ryan is playing at a dolls' house with two small stuffed, fabric dolls that he is attempting to dress. Concentrating on the tiny clothes, he sings freely to an 'aah' syllable sound. It is impossible to catch immediately everything that he sings, but sometimes he drones on one single pitch, sometimes there are snatches of a melody which sound like 'London Bridge is falling down', interspersed with strands of free-floating melody.

When playing alone, particularly with the fine-motor manipulation of doll-dressing, train-track linking or threading beads, Ryan sang long lines of rhythmically free-flowing melody on open vowel sounds. Sometimes this settled into snatches of melody, some which were recognisable as song melodies that he would have absorbed from prior experience.

Chanting

> On his own, Ryan sits on the floor playing with the train set. As he focuses on joining the links of the train set together he sings freely again. Alex, the early years practitioner in this room, is near by. 'Alex, A-A-A-lex,' chants Ryan quite loudly, singing on two notes, like a football chant. 'I'm playing with the train set,' says Ryan to him when Alex looks up.

Short verbal phrases were chanted on simple melodic ideas, very often as a kind of social call to other children or adults, as in this example of calling to Alex.

Reworkings of known songs

> The dolls chant 'hello' [to the same tune as the Hello song sung earlier]. 'It's stuck, eh, it's stuck, they is all squashed,' he says. A game of dolls trapped under dolls' house furniture continues. 'Err, err, err, err,' he says in the low-pitched, gruff timbre voice. 'Hello, poo poo da,' he sings to the melody and rhythm of 'Hello, everyone', which is the daily opening song for the formal singing session.

Ryan's word-changing to the familiar 'Hello, everyone' song, to 'Hello, poo poo da', reveals children's ability to transform and rework songs in their own play. All children enjoy changing song words enormously – it is a form of language play – particularly subverting the song words to something less reverent. If one purpose of singing is to dissipate tension, then word-changing may help this process.

There were two songs I recognised from Ryan's vocal play that day. This does not discount the possibility of more songs which I didn't know. 'London Bridge,' which he had sung earlier to the dolls' house game, I was certain of because sometimes he sang a few words. Mostly, however, he sang it to 'la'. Interestingly, it was not one of the circle-time songs which Alex ever included, so it must be a song from home. In another setting I spent much time observing an Arabic boy who had no English as yet but sang his way, almost continually, through the day. Without knowledge of Arabic songs how could I know what was reworkings of songs he had learnt and what was completely of his own making?

Movement vocalising

Ryan has moved to a table with laces and large wooden beads. Some are already threaded up. He stands, swinging a beaded lace back and forth so that it brushes the floor. 'Whee, whee, whee, whee,' he vocalises to match each swing of the beads.

Ryan throws one doll up high in the air, watching it rise and fall to the floor ahead of him in an arc. 'Up the choo!' he calls in a high pitch, rising curve, as he throws it. Five times he throws the doll up and calls 'Up the choo' each time. The 'choo' sound is lengthened and curls higher in pitch with each lob. Two dolls are thrown this time, twice, accompanied by 'chip-chop'. He takes a run and jumps, synchronising vocally, 'Choo!' and does the same movement again, 'Choo!'

This kind of vocal play falls into two types: vocalising to match his own movement or to match the movement of moving objects. In the throwing-dolls phase 'up the choo' exactly matches his lobbing of the little dolls in the air. This is followed by Ryan running and jumping and vocalising 'choo' as he jumps. It is particularly interesting in the second description that the dolls are thrown high and then Ryan throws himself in the air, going 'choo' in the same way. I have seen this many times, that children act out the movements of objects themselves but retain the same vocalisation for both.

Vocal drama

Ryan grips both dolls, one in each hand, holding them upright, and bounces them along the table surface, 'Aar, aar, aar, aar'. He talks in a low-pitched, gruff-timbred voice on behalf of one of the dolls: 'raar, raar, raar,' without specific words.

The dolls were given a low-pitched 'croaky' voice that, at a guess, was imitating the voice of an adult male. Children often role-play with dolls and animals and give them character voices with changes of vocal timbre. These sounds are usually intoned on single pitches or simple, expressive bends and twists of pitch. Often the sounds are repeated in small groupings of three or four.

Vocally imitating sounds

One doll fires noises at the other: 'Prr, prrr, prrr, prrr, aargh, prrr, prrr.' 'Boom, bosh, bosh!' calls out Ryan as one piece of wooden furniture is stamped on a doll. Furniture is piled, burying one doll. 'Ouch! I hurt myself,' calls the doll. But unrelentingly furniture continues to be piled on to the doll, 'Bong! Bong! Bong!'

Ryan's play is punctuated throughout with dramatic, comic-strip and cartoon noises, 'splash', 'brrr, brrr', 'ouch!' 'boom!' 'bang!' These are sharp bursts of energy accompanied by a matched acting out with the dolls and other toys.

What can be learnt from these observations?

Ryan is deeply involved in dramatic-music-movement play, playing with time and space in his own movement and the movement of objects. He is constantly shifting and transforming his ideas in their many sensory forms. When, for example, he swings the thread of beads back and forth he sees, feels kinaesthetically, 'sings' and hears the weight, the motion and the timing of that movement as an integrated whole. His vocalisation is one part of the whole experience.

In role play, he is exploring actions and emotions in simulated, dramatic situations. Both sets of processes, the transformations across different modes of ideas – or schema – which are structurally the same and the dramatising of simulated situations seem fundamental to young children's imaginative efforts. And within them vocalisations play an important part.

The vocal ideas can be understood not only as coming from 'within' Ryan but arise as much from the possibilities for play offered 'without', by the toys, the space and the people around him. The fabric dolls, for example, with which Ryan played, were just a size and weight to be lobbed about two metres in the air, the room high and spacious enough to allow this chucking activity and the adults around him providing a setting for him to play freely.

Sometimes it would seem that Ryan's vocal play takes centre stage in his attention. At other times, he is very intent on some other mode of activity and so the vocalisation is not the focus of his attention but a kind of subconscious activity. Sometimes two dimensions of activity, his vocal and physical play for example, are inseparable, at other times the integration of two modes is much weaker, so that two activities double-track alongside one another without seeming to be tightly integrated.

Finally, here is another example of a form of vocal play which I have noticed among other children but which wasn't part of Ryan's play that day.

Imitating singing style

> Danielle (four years one month) is playing with some domino shapes. Engrossed, she sings freely, improvising melodically. At one point she incorporates phrases from the 'Barbie Girl' song, singing 'I'm a Barbie Girl.' I notice she changes her singing tone to the nasal, American pop style of the recorded version of 'Barbie Girl'. At the same moment she pauses, domino in hand, standing a little upright, swaying from side to side.

Talking to her mother later, she tells me that Danielle has a toy cassette player with microphone and likes to use it to imitate her mother, who is a fitness trainer and uses a wide collection of CDs for her work. The 'Barbie Girl' song is from one of her favourite children's cassette tapes.

Danielle was imitating not just the rhythm and pitch details of the song and singing it in her own way, as Ryan did – she also imitated the style of performance, the way of using the voice and the dance movements which are a part of pop songs. Her singing play reflects absorbed experiences, from home and the wider musical culture. It resurfaced to be incorporated, momentarily, into her individual singing improvisation. She is playing with music but in the process is absorbing the idioms of popular music. At home, with different kinds of toys – the cassette player and microphone – she can play-sing the whole performance with movements and voice. She is entering a world by role-playing the singing and dancing of the performers.

Adults: joining in with voice-play

The early years practitioner in Ryan's playroom, Alex, joined in with his play at one point in a way which gives a model for how adults might join in with children's voice-play. During the session from which all the examples above were collected, he joined Ryan in a game of rolling cars down a ramp. He too vocalised 'wheee' and 'boom, bosh' in imitation of Ryan's vocal lead, yet at the same time he talked to Ryan about the activity. In this way he both drew out the playful quality of the car game and scaffolded his input around this play. Too often the adults in early years settings are busy with care tasks or leading the children in some way rather than being play partners, connecting with children's activity on their terms. What was also interesting is that Alex, in comparison with many early years practitioners, was very tolerant of noise and boisterousness on the part of the children. Free play which is vocally vibrant, engaging and energetic may well call for tolerance when indoors, or the more accommodating spaces outdoors.

Gabrielle Wicker, who runs sessions for toddlers and pre-schoolers with their carers in Cumbria, encourages adults to play interactively with singing and other vocalisations. She writes:

> in my sessions singing is not confined to songs; greetings, good-byes, instructions and stories are sung. Everyday toys, like teddies and puppets join in games. Parents are encouraged to play question and answer games using Play People and play-mats. Children go on make-believe expeditions, and sing what they see, hear, eat . . . life really does become an opera!
>
> (Wicker, 2002)

Meetha (three years seven months) sings a little snatch about 'going on the bus' as she does a jigsaw with Caroline. Caroline sang back a copy of her short phrase. Meetha looks up, stops the jigsaw for a moment and sings the phrase again. It develops into a turn-taking singing game.

All such song play and song-making comes easily to young children. The emphasis is on having fun together, on playing in a joky and light-hearted way with words and song forms and making a singing game. Caroline picked up the same pitch that Meetha first sang. In this way Meetha could hear her own singing reflected back to her, aurally, and the process of learning to be aware of pitch and to control pitch is supported.

Carers who spend long stretches of time with the children have the opportunity to pick up on singing and vocal play as it is integrated into other contexts. This is the advantage parents have at home. They will also be better equipped to recognise snippets of known songs which the children are reproducing in their play.

Rapid progress in singing at this age is associated with the amount of singing that takes place between child and adults, how their own singing is recognised and how much singing is modelled for them. Lucy's parents are both working as musicians, Kim as an early years music practitioner and Ian as an opera singer. Lucy not only accompanies Kim to many of her music sessions, she hears her father practise. She has a karaoke set, songbooks, videos and cassettes of songs. What's more, her singing is noticed, praised, encouraged – Kim and Ian sing with her, playfully, in many everyday situations. It is noticeable that Lucy already has a wide repertoire of songs, sings to herself when she plays and sings confidently with others.

Creating an environment for singing play

First and foremost, an environment which fosters singing play will have listening adults who are well tuned in to hearing and valuing children's spontaneous musical activity. It also strikes me that good internal spaces, light, airy rooms with quality flooring, are important for expressive, creative play. Whenever children find themselves in a free space they take advantage of the chance to run, dance, vocalise and sing.

Cars, trains and other small objects will stimulate free singing and a range of vocalisations as children play, particularly objects which suggest movement like vehicles, planes and animals. Vocal role play is also stimulated by puppets, soft toys and picture books which are 'sung', or have free vocalisations within the story. Laminated cards with picture and word prompts of the 'songs we can sing' can be displayed or used as reminders, both for adults and for children.

Puppets and soft toys can move, dance, role-play for singing and interact with the child. They can pick up the rhythmic movement of singing or swoop and dive to melody. Puppets who have open-and-close mouths (primarily intended for speech therapy) are particularly useful in that they can 'sing' too.

Tirzah Redman works in a day nursery in Penzance. An old cassette player which no longer works was stripped of batteries and leads and put in the role-play area. The children press the button on and then sing their own music and dance. One boy has language delay and doesn't yet talk – Tirzah saw him singing 'Twinkle' and trying to say the words. Another girl was dancing, and her mother, who works in the nursery recognised it as the way she dances to the radio in the kitchen at home.

One piece of equipment – an old cassette recorder – provided the catalyst for different kinds of singing activity. Ways of playing are then picked up among the children who play together and further transformed and developed.

Learning to sing songs

Children sing spontaneously and creatively but they also need to learn to join in with singing with others and learn to sing songs of their own culture and beyond. This process is supported by play-singing. Spontaneous vocal play supports the muscular control and the perceptual skills that help young children to learn to control their voices. In turn, by surrounding children with a lot of one-to-one singing in all kinds of situations, they develop a positive disposition towards singing and singing becomes part of everyday life. By play-singing with children, improvising songs and encouraging them to sing interactively, they develop an understanding of how songs work musically.

Children teach themselves to sing songs which they hear frequently around them, sometimes practising a current song with frequent repetitions. Over the course of a few weeks Sophie worked very hard to learn to sing the song shown on the next page. It was one Maureen often sang. It was not part of the usual repertoire for circle time but cropped up at drinks time, when the children asked for it or as part of free-play.

4 March. Sophie (three years one month) asks Maureen to sing this song for her. Maureen has to repeat it many times, putting in every name Sophie asks for. Playing on her own later, she sings to her dolls. 'Dolly, dolly' – this little first bit of the song over and over.

She moves over to Sam (another staff member) and asks her to sing 'Dolly, dolly' for her, standing directly over Sam, who

Jo - die, Jo - die, it's a lo - vely day.

Jo - die, Jo - die, come on out to play.

Jo - die, get your nap - pie on, tell Ay - i - sha we won't be long.

We'll be wait - ing round the cor - ner.

is sitting on the floor. Very intently she watches Sam – who, aware of this, sings it for her very slowly. Sophie is still watching her, so Sam sings it again and leaves out the last words of each phrase, cueing Sophie to complete: 'Sophie, Sophie, it's a lovely . . ., Sophie, Sophie, come on out to . . .'.

15 April. Sophie is playing with some dolls. 'Baby, baby, it's a lovely day, come on out to play.' The melody of the first two lines is a bit altered – and the language is not too clear. Sophie is practising both the language and the song. Later the same morning these first two lines come out more clearly. Later again, Sam and Sophie sing the first two lines together. Sam sings on and Sophie mouths and half-sings it.

13 May. During a free-play period Sophie spontaneously starts to sing 'Eleanor, Eleanor come on out to play!' This develops with various names. By now she can sing the first two lines of the song well, has a rough version of the next two lines and leaves out a section to end with 'round the corner'.

Interestingly, Sophie often starts the song on a different pitch but she can then continue and keep the song roughly in tune. Even the second phrase, which drops down a tone so that musically it is trickier to pitch in tune, she mostly pitches correctly. Irrespective of the order of words (she seems to sing the first and second line words interchangeably), she drops the pitch of the second phrase she sings. So it would seem that the musical order of phrases (a second phrase with matching melody line repeated a tone lower) has become more established than the sequence of word phrases. What can be learnt from these observations?

- The song is embedded in Sophie's everyday situations.
- She is remaking it for herself, constructing it bit by bit.
- It is sung for her when she asks, the adult obliges and happily follows her requests.
- The adult sings adapted versions of the song – adding names, singing more slowly – helping Sophie to join in.
- It begins to resurface, transformed and integrated into her play.
- She is very motivated to learn it, she works hard to learn from models and practises the song.

What can be interpreted in terms of Sophie's learning?

- She is drawn to this song because it fits her current needs and capabilities – musical, language, social, emotional.
- The song is meaningful because she can make it 'do' things for her – it can collect in and name the people around her and position her in a number of social networks (adults, family, siblings, peers). It helps her to negotiate the complex social and emotional fabric of pre-school and the shifts between home and elsewhere.
- She can use her singing voice with some control, she can sing the melodic shape of the song in the first line quite clearly and then can pitch the second line, which requires shifting down a note. If measured against strict versions of 'in-tuneness' she is not yet singing exactly in tune; her pitch-matching, like her pronunciation of words, is not yet exact and distinct.

Her singing ability is, incidentally, in advance of the expectations set out by developmental stages in children's singing. The difference, in my view, is that children's ability to learn to sing songs has mostly been 'measured' in formal song-learning situations rather than observed and analysed from informal, self-motivated song singing.

From this one example the following strategies to support song learning can be drawn out:

- Songs are sung for the child at their request and with contextual references as the child requires (references to familiar people, things and events).
- The song is sung very slowly for her as a model.
- Individual phrases are sung slowly, with pauses at key moments for her to contribute – maybe she is cued to sing the last word of each line, or to sing a key phrase.
- Singing continues on from her start or 'fills' any gaps.
- The adult shadow sings very quietly with the child.

Sophie was given the support to be a song-singer, to keep the lead, to play with the song in her own way. Like language learning, children learn by singing to and with people who sing with them, using songs in everyday contexts and connecting them with on-going activity. The song singing thus is purposeful, is meaningful to children.

So providing means by which children can weave songs into everyday life, and integrate them with toys, books, things they do, people and so on, is important. At home this may be always singing a song for going up the stairs, for hand-washing, for riding-in-the-buggy songs or in-the-car songs. It may be sitting together singing songs from a favourite rhyme and song book. Personalising songs by putting in the names of family members, or mentioning things known to the child. Making up new words to known songs or improvising ditties to fit with activities. An interest and enthusiasm for singing, for making songs your own, is much more important, in my view, than concern about the details of in-tune and in-time singing.

Semi-structured song activity

As part of the project we were interested to find ways of integrating song singing into the general play context of the nursery and to explore adult roles for being playful with songs. The staff in one setting evolved semi-structured play activities using songs as a starting point.

Anne planned and set up an activity around the song 'Five jellyfish'. A blue cloth was laid out on the floor for the sea, lots of plastic fish, jellyfish and other sea creatures. Fishing nets were set out and there were 'rocks' for the jellyfish to sit on. She sat on the floor ready to sing for children who chose to come, playing with the jellyfish and making them jump off the rocks. Part of the purpose was number work, as the number of jellyfish reduced one by one. But she also, skilfully, allowed the activity to develop in directions led by the children. Hannah and Casey jumped themselves into the blue sea and wanted Anne to sing for them when they were ready.

Next they both sat affectionately on her knee; she clutched them and 'wobbled' them on the 'jellyfish' when she sang it. Hannah stayed to play on, waving the fishing net about, popping it on Anne's head and then her own head as she sang bits of the jellyfish song to herself.

Notice how in this activity the initiative was shared. Anne took the lead sometimes but she did not have such a fixed plan that the activity could not divert to follow the initiatives introduced by the children. The song provided a frame for a role-play and number activity. The two girls who joined in also transformed the jumping jellyfish into their own jumping. Anne took their lead by singing the song for them when they requested it. They were, in this way, able to hear and experience the song matching their own movement. There was then a sociable, fun moment when the relationship between Anne and the children was affirmed with a cuddling lap game. Musically, the repetitions and active involvement in the song enabled Hannah to learn it successfully, as she then went on to sing it independently while continuing her play with the fishing net.

Collective singing session

Most nurseries include a collective singing session as part of their routine. During this session children hear and join in with a repertoire of songs and rhymes. The song singing may be included with a story – or separate from it. The children may be in smaller groups or gathered as one large group. Typically children are gathered together for a drink and snack time, and when sitting together the songs are included. Part of the purpose of such sessions is to prepare children for the more formal instruction of school and to begin to teach them to manage their behaviour in collective situations. Music's – or more precisely singing's – ability to bring people together is valuable for the way it draws everyone into a common activity.

While not wanting to diminish the informality and easiness of collective song singing, with all its social and musical benefits, there is some information about children's development as singers, some advice about strategies for helping children to sing and some thoughts about repertoire which can extend these benefits.

Physical capabilities for singing

In physical tasks it is common sense that their immature physical characteristics mean that young children may do the task quite differently from adults. We provide child-size equipment and adjust tasks to their capabilities. Just so with singing – but the physical differences are much less obvious. They have smaller lungs and breathe more frequently than adults. They may not have the lung capacity to be able to breathe across the longer phrases of songs – nor to sing very loudly. Asking children to sing up will only result in strained, 'shouty' voices and loss of pitch control. Helping them to sit up and think about breathing with lungfuls would be more constructive. But in comparison with adults, children's singing is quieter. Small group singing, in smaller spaces, may be more suited to the nature of children's singing.

Young children's vocal folds (vocal cords) are immature, softer and shorter. They may not have the vocal control to pitch-match as adults can. However, this does not mean that we should hold low expectations of children as singers. They are alert listeners, and – given good models, as with Sophie earlier in this chapter – can pick up the melodic detail of songs well. All too often I have observed lavish praise being given to children who seem barely engaged in the singing activity, let alone worthy of the praise. This surely gives confused messages. There may be a fear of denting children's confidence as singers by making higher demands, but they are served poorly by low expectations.

Repertoire

It is important to provide children with some songs which are vocally achievable for them to sing. Many of the traditional nursery repertoire, both old and more contemporary, are songs to sing *to* children. Just as there are stories to read to children and first activities which enable them to engage with literacy, similarly with songs. Many songs are ideal to sing for children. Their purpose may be to play a number game, to dance to, to celebrate an occasion, to provide richness of language. It is in keeping with the message of this book, to integrate musical activity in all kinds of playful contexts, that I would encourage lots of singing by adults, of many songs for many varying purposes. But if the aim is to help children to learn to sing songs, then some songs are more suited to the purpose than others.

Many nursery favourites lie outside pre-school children's current capabilities: the melodies are too wide-ranging and have tricky twists and turns. 'Five currant buns in a baker's shop' is an example. The phrases of the song are quite long. The melody starts low on 'Five', jumps quite a wide interval to 'currant buns' and then on 'baker's shop' jumps another wide interval. It also confusingly splits the word 'baker'. The next line of the song moves on to a new melody. In comparison, 'Ring-a, ring-a roses' sits on just three melody notes, it is made up of short snippets and the next line repeats the same tune. Interestingly, to refer back to the features of lullabies in Chapter 3 gives an almost exact list of the features of songs that would be helpful to young children learning to sing:

- The text is direct and related to children's lives.
- The song has a purpose, or is contextualised.
- There are no verses, the words are simple.
- The words keep one syllable to a note so that children can hear them clearly.
- The melody keeps to a narrow range of pitches.
- The intervals – the melodic leaps – are not too wide.
- The song is sung at a slow pace so that children can hear words and melody clearly.

I heard this next song (overleaf) being used by a nursery practitioner. She sang it with and to individual children when they were playing with instruments on the carpet area. She inserted the different names of the instruments as the children came up to her to play. It is a good example of a song which conforms with all the characteristics listed above.

There are some who advise a strict developmental approach to singing in which musical demands, the melodic and rhythmic

Ee-nie mee-nie min-ey mo!   I can hear those drum-mers go!

Looks so good, it sounds so fine!   Let me hear it one more time!

detail, are kept minimal at first and increased very gradually. As a result the song repertoire is confined to only those songs which young children are sure to sing 'successfully' in musical terms. In my view, there is so much more to singing than being concerned with children's ability to reproduce songs with vocal accuracy. Approaches based on introducing step-by-step songs which are developmentally appropriate are taking a narrow skills-based view of music and missing the social, communicative, the meaningful and expressive dimensions. On the other hand, taking care to select some repertoire which is appropriate to young children's developing capabilities as singers helps them to find the first footholds which might otherwise elude them. As in many things, it is a question of balance and breadth.

Learning purpose

Being clear on the range of learning purposes for song singing will support the process of selecting songs for more formal introduction at circle times. The following list suggests a number of purposes:

- to provide short rhythm or melody ideas for focused music learning;
- to provide a source for learning about other musical elements such as dynamics, pulse;
- to develop singing skills;
- to support rhythmical counting;
- to develop phonic awareness;
- to tell mini-stories;
- to accompany group role plays;

- to accompany dance movement, action games or ring games;
- to stimulate fine motor actions e.g. finger-play.

Some of these purposes are orientated towards music, some towards other areas. Songs are a rich and valuable resource for many kinds of learning.

Play-songs

The continuation of play-songs from earlier childhood form an important part of the repertoire. In pre-school settings they tend to lose their one-to-one, interactive character and change to become adult-led to small-group. Action and game songs are then modelled for the children to imitate. The predominance of action songs in the early years repertoire needs thinking about. On the one hand, music is a multimodal experience, particularly for young children, and so it suits their ways of being musical to integrate movement and visualisation through action with singing. The movements often pick up the rhythmic features of the song, the steady beat or a rhythm pattern, and so serve to underscore the musical dimensions. Actions often help to give the meaning of the song, which might otherwise be confusing or abstract to the children. Taking another view, however, I sometimes feel that the actions become a substitute for the singing itself and that the uniform participation they ensure has become their main value. Certainly most children will attempt the actions first and then attend to the details of the song words and melody. If the actions are complex, they will detract from anything else. One useful approach is to keep actions simple, repetitive and rhythmically close to the song.

Varying the pace of an action song can help children to learn to co-ordinate actions with words and melody. Very often the pace at which a movement can best be performed (and remember that children's body size means that this is often differently paced from adults) is not the pace at which a song can best be sung. The movements will tend to move quite quickly and children sing most successfully when the pace is slow.

Many action songs in early years involve small-scale finger and hand movements, often quite intricate. To perform these is quite a different experience (with different challenges) from the whole-body movements of ring games and dance singing games. Whole-body, dance movements enable children to receive a strong impulse of rhythmic movement and they enjoy managing their whole selves in co-ordinations of time. In terms of what they gain, larger-scale movements provide a much richer learning experience in music and dance than small body-part movements.

Such bigger movement activities, however, introduce challenges of control: stopping, direction, slowing down, staying still, being aware of others. First activities might need to focus on these skills, as in this song.

Up, up, up we   jump to - ge-ther.   Up, up, up we   jump and, STOP!

Finally

This chapter has focused mainly on one dimension of musical activity among pre-school children, all that they can do with their voices. The next chapter is its partner, staying with the same age phase and focusing on play with instruments and other sound-makers.

Chapter 8

On to three and then four

(II) Playing instruments

This chapter will look at:

*   self-initiated music-making on instruments
*   adults: joining in with instrumental music-making
*   providing for play with instruments

In this chapter we will look in detail at young children's music-making with instruments. Children derive great pleasure and satisfaction from playing instruments and finding their own ways of making music. But it can be easy to look upon this strand of activity as merely a source of fun, a relatively low-level activity of free, exploratory play. As with spontaneous singing in the previous chapter, careful observation will reveal the detail, the organisational thinking that lies behind young children's music and the ways in which it blends and integrates with other forms of activity. Once these processes become clear it gets easier to imagine ways of extending and developing children's music made with instruments. Like earlier chapters, this one will begin by looking at the ways children play instruments when left to their own devices and then at how adults can join in with and connect with their play.

Self-initiated music-making on instruments

As with spontaneous singing, children's music play with instruments integrates and blends with many other kinds of play.

The possibilities of the instrument

Jo-jo (three years two months) finds all the chime bars set out on a carpet outdoors. She arranges them neatly in a row, then plays up and down with one beater. She takes another beater and listens to the sound of two beaters playing simultaneously, then each hand alternately.

The instrument itself has certain possibilities and certain limitations which channel children's play. It is important, therefore, to give much thought to providing instruments which have rich potentials for play. This we will return to later in the chapter.

Body movement vocabulary

> Craig (four years) starts by swishing both beaters horizontally across the xylophone surface. Then he dabs very quickly with both hands together. Suddenly he swings both beaters up high with arms outstretched and, after a pause, crashes both down on to the keys.

In this example, which is typical, the playing actions take centre stage. The children explore the range of movements and enjoy the physical action of playing and hearing the sound that results. By observing carefully it is usually possible to see how their playing is organised as sequences and patterns of bodily movement.

Pathways

> Jasmine (three years six months) has set out an array of instruments on the floor around her. First she plays each instrument in turn, clockwise. She does this again several times. Then she plays them in reverse order.

Making patterns and pathways which are predominantly visual and spatial is a common feature of children's play in many different domains, not just in music play with instruments. While it can sound random, looking closely will reveal the logic underlying it.

Song

> Megan (three years two months) has a xylophone outside and is striking it rhythmically with one beater. As she does so she sings 'Humpty Dumpty' to coincide with her beats.

Often, playing the instrument gives the impetus for a song, usually a very familiar song, to resurface. The instrumental play and the song almost always synchronise rhythmically.

Number

Nathan (three years three months) counts up the xylophone keys one at a time, striking each one regularly in turn.

Here the visual layout of the instrument suggests a game of logic and regularity: counting each note in turn.

Dance

Isan (three years eleven months) has a tambourine and circles on the spot, holding one arm outstretched with the tambourine in his hand. He curves the tambourine up high and down low as he rotates.

Instruments which are pick-up-and-play allow children to move around freely while they play, often making up sound dances as they do so.

Drama

Ben (three years five months) holds two beaters upright like small puppets and joggles them at a steady pace on the top of a drum. 'Along the road, along the road,' he says simultaneously and then continues to act out a long mini-drama involving the two puppet beaters and the sounds he can produce with the drum.

Role play with instruments mostly appeared when the children could play quite alone and in peace. The instrumental playing serves to underscore aspects of the story and to provide sound tracking.

Performance model

Isobel (four years three months) has arranged a whole set of drums around her on the floor. She has taken two sticks and plays the drums 'kit style' in imitation of pop drummers.

Children played drums, made pretend keyboards and held beaters as microphones in imitation of models of performers they have seen on television or video. All influences are absorbed and remade in their own play. Pop music is an important influence, and in the previous chapter on vocal play we saw how Danielle imitated pop-style performance in her singing.

General processes

These descriptions of different kinds of play are intended to be a guide for looking at and becoming aware of how children are making their own music. They arose from one set of observations, of one group of children, in one nursery, by one person. But there are likely to be some commonalities here with the way most children compose. Although within these common approaches each child will bring individualities: one will always want a certain drum, another has an idea on the xylophone to which they always return, another is timid and finds it difficult to play freely. With most children, once an idea begins to generate their instrumental play – perhaps a movement idea, a visual/spatial idea – they usually repeat it several times, to re-experience it, to enjoy it, to listen to the sound that results.

However, there are some individual ways of playing instruments that just need thinking about. When first encountering them, some children produce very repetitive playing actions, usually just striking the instrument at a medium tempo in what can seem a very dull, almost mechanical, way. This kind of playing seems to arise from a need to minimise demands and create predictability, in a new, unfamiliar, perhaps unnerving situation. Although it may continue for a surprisingly long period of time – and seem unproductive – it produces a kind of stability from which children can then move on.

Sometimes difficult to cope with, however, are the few children for whom the instruments seem to trigger a need to play insistently and very loudly. The simultaneous action and sound which is possible when playing some instruments is a powerful medium which plugs in directly to the emotions. I have found that joining in with playing helps some to find self-controls and boundaries, although a very few may need expert help in learning to regulate their emotions. On the other hand, the sheer thrill of loud sounds is hugely exciting and stimulating. There are many kinds of loud, exhilarating music – pop music is characteristically high-volume, street bands can deafen, drummers can be ear-splitting. Like bright splashes of colour painting, of leaping off the climbing frame, we perhaps need to find ways of accommodating these high-energy, high-sensory experiences just sometimes. We tramped far away over the grass to crash the brilliant-sounding, shiny cymbals.

Beyond repetitions of ideas, children characteristically group single beats and strikes into small groupings, or clusters. These usually fall into regular lengths – most typically the grouping of seven regular beats found in 'Twinkle, twinkle'. There is some suggestion that these groupings, played as short clusters, then a pause, then again, represent characteristic and universal rhythmic forms which are to be found in children's rhymes. In my view, it is more likely that children have absorbed regular phrasing structures which occur in speech and music.

Once children had found one playing idea, and had played it repetitively for a while, they often began to transform it. They might extend the playing idea by adding something to it, change the pace by slowing it down or getting quicker, play it again but getting louder each time, add bits to it, reverse a pathway or change a movement shape. Notice that these are the same transformation processes which adults intuitively introduce into the singing games of babyhood.

> Rochenda (three years six months) played the xylophone in groups of seven strikes up from the bottom and then down from the top. She did this several times over. Then she paused, and changed to playing one note at a time and counting out the keys. Once she reached the top, she went back to the first idea of strikes up and down, but this time made the final strike very much stronger and louder.

As their play episode continues, children might return to the first idea and begin to blend ideas into other transformation and variations.

The music play of the three- and just-four-year-olds I observed and studied in a nursery very much progressed in a sequencing of ideas. By watching and listening carefully it was often possible to identify the kinds of ideas and processes underpinning their play. Far from being the disorderly, exploratory and almost chaotic play as is often suggested of young children, there are forms of organisation. But the ways children are organising and structuring their music-making come to the surface only if we see their instrumental play in terms which make sense to young children. If we search for coherent melodic shapes, rhythm patterns and so on, which are characteristic of adult-made music, they are likely to be absent – or at least difficult to pick out except in a few instances.

Adults: joining in with instrumental music-making

In my general observations of the way in which instrumental play is provided for in early years settings, there is little play *with* children by adults. In general, musical instruments are set out in one area with the expectation that children will play there freely with no adult intervention.

Listening and responding

Children get clear messages in early years education as to which activities are higher-status and carry more value. These are the ones set out on tables, in the centre of the room, with adults in attendance to support and guide. It has to be said that these are usually the activities which have a literacy or numeracy focus, reflecting the current pulls towards the formal curriculum which are influencing early years practice.

> Sylvie, one of the nursery practitioners, comes over to sit on the decking outside with some children who are playing groups of chime bars. 'Oooh, let me hear you,' she says. They play her some music. Sylvie sings along – a half made-up, half remembered song about 'raindrops' – and jiggles her hands in a dancing way to join in.

If adults attend to children's play with instruments, arrive to listen, take an interest and respond, then it conveys that this is a valued activity.

Joining in

In one nursery we experimented with different ways of setting out the instruments. On some days, just a xylophone or a collection of hand drums or a basket of small percussion instruments was set out on the carpet area. An adult sat at the instruments 'ready to play'. Children who came were given an opportunity to settle into playing and, if judged appropriate, the adult would join in with copying. A simple strategy of joining in by playing what the child did – or as near a copy as was possible – developed the play with children in sequences of turn-taking and playing simultaneously. It is a simple strategy for taking an active part in the child's music play and showing genuine involvement.

Information was systematically collected as part of a research project to measure how long the children played when an adult was play partnering and how long they played when adults completely ignored them (Young, 2000). We also compared a familiar adult who had no formal musical training and a relatively unfamiliar adult who did. As might be expected, the children played for the longest periods, and in more interesting and varied ways, when partnered by a familiar adult. They played for the shortest lengths of time when adults paid no attention and for longer times with the unfamiliar adult, but not as generously as with the adult they knew well. So, by partnering children in simple echo and match games, the nursery staff extended the quality and length of time the children played. Significantly, knowing the children well, and being experienced at playing with them, counted for more than formal music training.

In a further, interesting experiment as part of the same study, adults attempted to 'play badly' with the children in various ways. One adult directed the children, telling them how to hold the beaters, how to strike the notes cleanly and issued instructions such as 'play it like this'. This had an immediate effect in closing down the children's interest and confidence in their own playing. Another adult joined in with turn-taking but made little attempt to play 'like the children', instead playing musically conventional melodies and rhythm patterns when it was her turn. Again, the children lost interest and the play episode soon floundered. Finally, a version of 'bad playing' was tried in which the adult mistimed her turns, either leaving too long a gap or coming in too soon. Again, the child became frustrated with the adult partner. These experiments showed how subtle playing well with children can be and how valuable it was to pick up on the children's ideas and reflect them back in turn-taking. All the adults in the nursery play-partnered the children successfully in musically creative ways. The reason being that it relies on the same intuitive musical communicative processes that we apply in human interactions at all levels (Young, 1999).

Semi-structured play: adults and children together

An important strand of the project was to experiment with different groupings and ways of organising music activity in early years settings. One of the models we developed was semi-structured group activity. The aim was to develop musical activity in which adults participate with children but allow them to retain a measure of freedom and control. We had in mind approaches which lay between the adult-led, collective sessions and the child-led free play with instruments. These activities would take place during the main time of the nursery morning, not the circle-time slot. For semi-structured instrumental play it was usual to take a small selection of untuned percussion into an adjoining room. We found that a small selection of hand-held instruments worked well. The children joined the activity of their own choice – to a maximum of about six. The activity would develop from leads given either by the children or by the adult. Usually the adult had a song or music game in mind but would either wait for children's ideas before introducing it or, if leading the activity with the song, would then allow it to develop according to the children's participation. In one of these play episodes the children found a broken puppet on strings and improvised its dancing music around the room. In another, the adult copied some rhythm patterns one played and they spent some time trying to play these on different instruments. Much time was spent inspecting the percussion, trying it out, talking about the different sounds and ways of playing.

'Leads' by the adult were:

• introducing songs with 'play-alongs';
• modelling playing techniques such as how to hold or strike;
• modelling rhythm patterns;
• modelling getting different dynamic sounds from the instruments, different qualities of sound;
• instructing how to play in certain ways or participate in certain guided ways.

'Follows' by the adult were:

• listening to the children and observing, showing an active interest;
• playing another instrument with them; copying, playing something which fits but is different;
• dancing with the children's play;
• making a puppet or toy dance to their playing or vice versa;
• commenting on their playing, talking about the instruments and their playing of them with the children.

Adult-initiated and led

In larger-group, more formal sessions the adult leads the activity. The children typically have one instrument each – sticks, egg shakers, bells – or an instrument which is easily sharable – a gathering drum which all the children could stand around, or an instrument the children pass to play by turn.

Integrating the instrument playing with songs and actions provides a structure and framework for their playing. In larger-group activity, the self-control to hold instruments still and to be quiet becomes a necessary skill to learn. Short practice activities are useful such as : 'Shake, and shake, and shake, and STOP!'

Well known action rhymes such as:

Roll 'em, roll 'em, up, up, up,
Roll 'em, roll 'em, down, down, down.
Roll 'em, roll 'em, clap, clap, clap,
Put your hands behind your back.

can be adapted for instruments – here with sticks.

Tap them, tap them, up, up, up [only tap them on the
      'up, up, up']
Tap them, tap them, down, down, down.
Tap them, tap them, tap, tap, tap [or one, two, three],
Put your sticks behind your back.

Providing for play with instruments

Children are so motivated to play instruments, and often play them so exuberantly and boisterously, that it can seem like the most valuable aspect. And in one way it is. Pity the moment when everything focuses down on to narrow educational priorities and loses sight of the fun, the pleasure of this moment now. However, moving on from seeing the enjoyment children derive to consider carefully what they are gaining is important in making decisions about how instrumental play will be provided for.

Perhaps one of the reasons that music activity with instruments seems less well developed in early years contexts in comparison with singing is that it is more difficult to tease out the learning gains. With singing, more of the gains can be identified as broad, general aims to do with learning to be a member of a group, extending language and so on. With instrumental play, there *can* be broader-based benefits, but the main gains are centred in music. They are to:

- listen and discover a wide range of different sound qualities and tuned and untuned sounds;
- develop a range of techniques for producing sounds;
- play with very free, movement-based rhythms – around instruments which are fixed in one place, or moving around with sound-makers;
- play a steady beat – alone or synchronising with another;
- play rhythmic patterns – starting with spontaneous rhythm patterns and picking up on rhythm patterns from others;
- play short melodic ideas (on tuned percussion) – usually from a pattern on barred instruments;
- repeat short musical ideas and link ideas into sequences;
- play in phrases – by grouping repetitive beats or playing longer rhythmic phrases.

Doing these things alone, in turn-taking or matching with others represents different sets of skills. I have suggested that adults picking up on children's ideas gives children the experience of hearing and feeling someone else fitting in with their music-making. Through this process the children hear their ideas played back to them. This is much the same process which adults use when helping children to talk. The child says something which is a little unformed and the adult, trying to make sense of it, repeats it back to them. The children retain the initiative, the music-making is on their terms, but they experience playing, singing or moving in harmony with someone else. The usual demand made of young children, to match what someone else gives them, to co-ordinate their singing, their playing, their moving with an external model – is a much harder skill and one which develops slowly and with time.

What instruments?

There is such a wide range of instruments available that selecting equipment for an early years setting can present dilemmas. The different types of instruments available highlight the confusion about where young children's music fits in.

- Early education versions of toys; bright, robust plastics, animal faces and, in general, a poor sound. Variations and developments of rattles of babyhood, shaker-type instruments.
- Early education versions of educational percussion instruments designed for work with older children. Usually in natural, varnished wood. Some adaptations for young children such as smaller size, shorter beaters.
- Specifically designed early education percussion, for example the Montessori music equipment.
- Imported ethnic instruments, usually hand-made in natural materials.
- Derivations of special needs instruments where thought has been given to how small hands will hold and play, or arrangements of instruments clipped on to stands.

Various considerations, of safety, of what is robust and cannot hurt, and of cost, among suppliers mindful of limited budgets have further influenced the choice of materials and design of instruments, but not always with concern for the quality of sound the instruments make. There is an aesthetic implicit in many children's instruments of a cheerful, plastic, throw-away, 'things to bash' music which does not serve well the aural imaginations of children. The six-month-old who will be immobile, listening to the clink of a treasure basket chain, becomes the three-year-old who hasn't lost that fragile sensitivity to beauty of sound. Good quality of sound is a priority, to be aimed for over and above quantity.

There is also the idea that small people need small instruments. Unfortunately, the timbre and pitch of small instruments tend to be limited to higher pitches and low resonance. Small instruments are useful for pick-up-and-hold activities, but free-standing static instruments can be larger, deep-sounding and resonant.

Thinking about the play potential of instruments also influences choice. One chime bar may have limited play potential but a small set of chime bars with several beaters made of different materials generates all kinds of possibilities for two-handed patterns, patterns in and between the different bars, steps up and down, repeated rhythm patterns on each bar in turn – and all these with the different sound qualities produced with a change of beaters.

Play, listen and explore sound qualities

Those equipping early years settings with instruments will want to ensure that the range of instruments provided covers a wide variety of different sound qualities – for example, resonant, bell-like sounds, wooden, skin sounds, dry, rattly sounds – and that there are varieties of pitch, including some tuned instruments. Play and listen can be encouraged in the following ways:

• The adult models play the instruments and encourages children to listen very attentively, talking about the sounds, during a circle time, or an adult-led table activity.
• Instruments are set out in a large box, or tent – children enter and listen only one at a time.
• The adult introduces listening games where the instruments are hidden, under a cloth, in bags or boxes, and encourages children to listen carefully.

Play and move rhythmically

Some instruments which are pick-up-and-play or wearable prompt simultaneous play and dancing among children. However, these activities do need space, either indoors or out-of-doors.

Play out a steady beat, play rhythm patterns

Playing a steady beat, regular tapping or drumming I have always found to be absolutely basic to all children, something they can do without difficulty. More important is to ensure that the physical demands of playing the instrument allow them to play easily – all too often they are struggling with over-large tambourines, heavy, awkward triangles or some such. Connecting in with their steady beat playing, synchronising with it, is a pleasing experience for all children. Then, once they are playing steadily, add a rhyme or song, so that they can hear how the next musical layer is fitting. By this method, the child is setting the pace which suits them best.

Play on the drum, play on the drum,
Rumpety, tum, rumpety tum.
Play on the drum, play on the drum,
Rumpety, tumpety, rumpety tum.

Play and develop techniques for making sound

Most instruments provided in early years settings are percussion instruments requiring relatively simple playing techniques such as shake, tap or scrape. Striking with a beater or a hand, two beaters or both hands, introduces more possibilities. The movements for shaking some of the larger instruments can be quite difficult to co-ordinate. Grip and tap instruments may need some time for practice. Stands to hold instruments are very useful and have the advantage of fixing instruments in one place. The stands can be purpose-built or improvised. On drums, playing with hands is more tactile and produces less noise, but the drums need to be good-quality and to produce a resonant sound. Providing a range of beaters in varying materials – plastic, wood, rubber, felt – extends the range of sound possibilities which can be obtained.

Blown instruments are often avoided because of concerns about health and hygiene. But as an adult-guided, occasional activity they considerably extend the range of instrumental play. Many children have pipes and whistles at home, and an interesting collection can be assembled. Similarly, stringed instruments which are plucked introduce another whole vista of sound possibilities – guitars, zithers, violins. Music technology opens up another range of instrumental sounds. From the simple footpads available from children's toyshops to keyboards, multimedia systems and sensory equipment available for special needs children, there is a wealth of equipment which can produce exciting sounds with minimal technical skill.

Instrumental set-ups

Early years settings plan the environment and how equipment will be set out. This includes the allocation of adults to the set-ups. In creating set-ups for instrumental play there are decisions to be made about:

- *Where?* On tables (for focused play), floor, outside, in an open space.
- *For how long?* Specific time slots, or throughout the whole session?
- *What?* Selected instruments set out.
- *How?* They are integrated with e.g. role play, recorded music, puppet play.
- *Who* will act as a listener, observer, play partner?

Using instruments can raise a number of concerns about noise, about children playing them in a way which appears to be 'just messing about'. Varying the set-ups and, in particular, setting a selection out on tables or carpet area with an adult in attendance can result in the children playing the instruments in a more focused and controlled way.

Outdoor instruments

Providing for instrument play out-of-doors works well. From pop festivals to street bands, much of the world's music is made out-of-doors. The noise dissipates in the open spaces. It may be almost unreasonable to expect to accommodate certain instruments with louder sounds in smaller indoor spaces. Instruments can be set up outside temporarily, on rugs or tables, or permanent outdoor music-play structures constructed.

Adult performers

Adults playing with children in music with instruments has been the main focus of this chapter. What also works very well is for adults who have their own instrumental skills, probably on one main instrument, or possible a few, to play with children. The children join in by playing the adult instrument, one of their own or by singing.

Joy is a parent helper visiting the nursery for one morning who has specialist skills as a pianist. She sits at the piano in a nursery hallway with children one by one on her lap. Joy plays for children who join in, adding their own singing and playing contributions as she plays. Sometimes Joy changes what she is playing, and improvises to fit in with the children, sometimes she continues to play a composed piece.

Finally

Having moved progressively through different ages and different kinds of musical activity, chapter by chapter, it is now important to focus on the role of the music practitioner. The final chapter considers aspects of the role but will promote the idea of reflective practice in which practitioners analyse their work around a number of different frameworks.

Chapter 9

Reflective practice

This chapter will consider:

* questioning practice
* methods for observing
* frameworks for questioning practice
* review and revision

The purpose of this final chapter is to focus on the role of the early years practitioner in music and in particular to focus on the idea of reflective practice. This incorporates the processes of collecting information about musical activity in all its forms, analysing the information to deepen understanding and, on the basis of that understanding, reviewing and planning for change and improvement. All this in the belief that the quality of music with under-fours will be best served by a creative blend of deep-thinking, honest evaluation and openness to fresh ideas.

Most work in early years music is now subject to evaluation by outside agencies, either directly from funding organisations or indirectly as part of the evaluation procedures applied generally to early years provision. In this kind of evaluation the questions are already fixed, or at least held implicitly in the way the procedures are set up. Thus there are likely to be two sides to evaluation, internal and ongoing, as part of the development of good practice, and external and final, as part of a process of accountability to others. How can the two fit together and benefit one another?

Questioning practice

Evaluation, as part of accountability to outside funders or as part of a general overview of provision, can be a powerful influence on the direction and working practices of early childhood music practitioners. Outside agencies ask questions about numbers, ages of children, demographic detail, practical information concerning the work itself, much of it with the emphasis on providing evidence of 'success' and targeting high numbers of children, particularly those considered to be in particular need. While these questions may lift quality, expand opportunity and help to even out disadvantage, they can also fail to get at what really matters. The significant changes are not likely to be found in simple measurable information. They are to be found in the actions of individual children and carer–child pairs when they are engaged in musical activity. It is getting inside, questioning, these small-scale, complex details – yet not so small-scale in terms of what they tell us – that will provide rich and valuable information and begin to indicate what is working successfully and what less so. This kind of quality experience-based information will accumulate in the ongoing processes of observing, analysing and reflecting on practice. It should be possible for these processes to give rise to deeply informative accounts of work which can then be a valuable resource for outside evaluators.

There is increasing emphasis on providing evidence of quick-return value, but longer-term change and benefits may accumulate from slower developments in awareness, knowledge and increase in skills. Such long-term development may well arise from work which has less to show on the surface. To demonstrate 'value' for music work practitioners may be tempted to build in high-visibility outcomes, final celebratory performances which may not well represent the nature of the work. Careful thought might suggest alternative forms of celebration, such as process diaries of staff, musical stories of individual children or written accounts by participating parents describing longer-term impacts of the work. And when aims and purposes may have been carefully designed to suit local situations and their values and priorities, broad-brush, general criteria requested by external bodies can rarely be fine-tuned to demonstrate 'success' against the stated aims of a project. Reflective practice might empower practitioners to present their own locally determined criteria together with information to demonstrate progress and development.

External evaluation procedures cannot directly and actively guide the professional development of individual practitioners. They can even undermine valuable processes of honest self-review because of the need, in some cases, to report successes to ensure continued income. Practitioners working in early years may be connected with larger organisations such as Sure Start networks, local education authorities, regional arts organisations, community music, music services, health arts, but even within these they may be working largely in an isolated and independent way. Without networks of other practitioners it can be difficult to self-evaluate, review and identify own needs for professional development. There is no national system of accreditation for early years music, and many people with a range of training and experience are extending the scope of their work into the rapidly expanding area of early years. Without at least some common frameworks of practice, it is even more important that practitioners seek to develop their work through self-initiated processes of reflection.

Self-questioning

Reflective practice is, fundamentally, the habit of critical thinking. It starts with self-questioning, becoming conscious first of our own culture and background experiences in a very real and practical sense, and how these impinge on all that we do. It includes being clear on our assumptions and beliefs about music and early childhood, both in how we see young children themselves and the adult roles of caring and educating them. Talking openly within networks of other professionals helps to throw into relief the ideas and attitudes we hold. The process of reflective practice begins, then, here with ourselves.

Observing and documenting practice

Throughout this book I have emphasised that a heightened awareness of the child's own music-making will lead to a stronger appreciation of the abilities and potentials which young children bring. This in turn will lead to changes in the ways we work. The influence of the Italian pre-schools known as Reggio Emilia has shown the value of observing and documenting the processes of children's play (Edwards *et al.*, 1995). By documentation the staff of the Reggio Emilia schools have in mind more than collecting just what can be seen and heard. They also track in detail the responses of children to the initiations and interventions of adults. Their purpose is continually to question the processes of children's learning in interaction with the adults working with them. In a similar way, I have provided descriptions of observations followed by my interpretations. My aim was to model active listening and watching, together with pondering how adult actions have been part of the process. And, importantly, to show how part of ordinary everyday and fleeting many of the most significant moments can be, particularly with the very youngest children.

I have argued that all too often music with young children can be all about the adults as the active 'doers', with little effort to get inside the child's experience, to understand what the children are doing and gaining. If initiating activity in music, as those working in music are often required and expected to do, it is very difficult to be simultaneously alert to the responses of the children. It is key, therefore, for practitioners to have time out to observe children in general play activities, playing in environments designed for music or to play in semi-structured musical activity with children on a one-to-one or a one-to-a-few basis. Setting aside time to listen to children's spontaneous music-making and seeing this as an essential and intrinsic part of the work may represent a fundamental change of role. Those who are used to being visibly active in music may find the change of role difficult to justify to themselves – and to others also. It is often the case that musical identity is tied up with being the one who is visible as the performer-entertainer, and shifting this may require giving up a rewarding dimension of the role.

Methods of observing

Very young children's musical behaviours can be so embedded in all else that is going on that it is understandably difficult to know what one is aiming for and what it looks and sounds like when you have it. It doesn't lend itself to being separated out and there are few ways of satisfactorily collecting it up.

In practical terms, observation can be a simple process of sitting quietly close by children and tuning in. Sometimes it was only by crouching at toddler level that I could even hear that they were singing. I thought I was quite good at it. But the acute technologically assisted ears of the sound recordist working with the film crew picked up singing that I was not aware of and showed me that there was even more going on than I had thought. Like any active listening, it requires concentration and attempting to bring everything to a level of conscious awareness. It is by no means easy to maintain a high level of awareness and alertness in order to see and hear the detail of children's music. Writing notes, jotting down everything seen and heard, can be a useful way to keep focused. However, I find that the moment I start writing I stop listening and watching. Nevertheless, it is important to try to collect the detail of children's music play by some means so that it can be reviewed, discussed and analysed at a later point. Methods of collecting information about children's music play can include:

- freely written notes – by practitioner, parent, carer;
- more structured observation sheets – which set out time slots, certain specific behaviours to look for or certain children to track;
- video recording;
- cassette recording;
- photographs.

On another level, as I have emphasised, observing is about setting aside preconceived ideas of what music sounds like in an adult world and tuning in, literally, to the child's ways of being musical. Much research into very young children's musical behaviours has focused on narrow sets of musical skills and features, the pitch range of children's singing voices or the kinds of rhythms they characteristically first play on instruments, for example. Such focuses and analyses miss the way that musical behaviours are woven into play. It is more fruitful, and more in keeping with our understandings of how children play, learn and progress, to attempt to understand music as one facet of general play and how it is tied into surroundings of people and things. It is this shift in perspective, developing the ability to imagine the real, embedded, musical experiences of the children – or at least endeavour to as best we can – that is crucial.

Video recording

Capturing children's musical activity, and adults interacting with children, on video provides one of the best means of review and reflection on practice. So it is valuable to look at this method in more detail.

Static set-ups, such as an arrangement of instruments or an adult working in one position with children who cluster, can be captured on video recording relatively easily. In one nursery I simply jammed a small camera on a tripod behind a small upholstered chair and left it running for the length of the video film (approximately an hour). Although sometimes filming no children at all, or at other times small fingers exploring the lens, it gave an overall record of the children's play in one area set up with some percussion instruments. On another occasion we hand-held the camera at a distance to avoid distraction and used the zoom lens to capture the detail of children's play. Needless to say, permission from parents needs to be sought if children are to be video-filmed and the purpose of the filming made clear to them.

Asking others to film your own practice can lead to important insights. A group of practitioners on an early years music course were asked to video-record aspects of their work and evaluate it. Once they had got past the cringe factor of watching themselves on video replay, they found the experience enlightening. They learnt even more from the process of coming together to view and discuss their video recordings. These practitioners commented that it was difficult to get past looking at themselves to focus on how the children were participating. But they added that they were often surprised to find that what they thought had been happening as they worked with the children was not borne out by the video evidence. Another practitioner was frustrated that the filmer had selected aspects of her work to record which she did not consider the most valuable. This led to a conversation about observation as selective: even video recording is not capturing the whole picture but a biased view.

They also found that replay of video recording can be very time-consuming and analysis of mixed and multimodal activity can be tricky, but concluded that the way in which video recording captures the rich detail and enables repeat reviewing outweighs the disadvantages. This group of practitioners found that knowing what to look for was difficult at first, but as they reviewed the video recording several times over, new things began to surface.

Frameworks for questioning practice

It is possible to observe the children and just let a trail of interest develop which you then follow. Some like doing observation this way, as it can lead to new discoveries. But frameworks are useful at all stages of reflective practice – for organising what is already known, for deciding and guiding what to observe, for analysing information collected and for planning how practice might move on. What follows are a number of different frameworks for conceptualising music with under-fours. They are intended to emerge from the descriptions and discussion of the book – and also to be adaptable to a variety of situations. They are not prescriptive but intended to support the process of asking questions within reflective enquiry.

Investigating young children's musical experiences

Observation might track one kind of activity among under-fours:

* spontaneous vocalisation as part of general play;
* self-initiated music play with sound-makers and/or instruments;
* spontaneous response to recorded music;
* rhythmic movement as part of general play;
* participation in songs sung to babies/toddlers/children and when they are learning songs;
* ability to reproduce songs they are learning;
* participation in instrumental activity which is guided by adults;
* ability to reproduce rhythmic movements modelled for them;

or track one kind of activity across a number of different ages. For example: how do one-year-olds, two-year-olds and three-year-olds respond to recorded music? Or it might focus on certain children:

* one child for a period of time and track all forms of musical activity;
* a small group engaged in one semi-structured activity;
* children from a similar ethnic or cultural background.

Investigating the adult role

The whole spectrum of ways in which adults can interact with children in music provides a useful frame for evaluating practice as it is now and for exploring alternative approaches. It will be most valuable if an investigation into adult roles is accompanied by an investigation into the effect of adult roles on the nature of the child's experience.

- *Observing and listening*
  - not participating directly, focusing on children's self-initiated activity when alone or in interaction with another adult carer.
- *Responding non-verbally*
  - showing active listening and noticing – with positive facial expressions, vocal expressions and by body movement;
  - managing and supporting an activity, e.g. positioning the child and/or objects within reach.
- *Responding verbally*
  - giving positive comments and encouragement;
  - introducing vocabulary for talking about music.
- *Imitative play partnering*
  - child takes the lead, adult picks up on their contributions, imitating;
  - setting up turn-taking, using the children's ideas.
- *Contributory play partnering*
  - child takes the lead, adult picks up on their contributions;
  - setting up turn-taking, using the children's ideas, but adult extends, adds to or modifies slightly.
- *Semi-structured play partnering*
  - adult or child taking the lead. Adult may model, providing new input, or imitating and following. Lead or follow roles changing flexibly within play episode.
- *Lead play partnering*
  - adult initiating activities but leaves 'spaces' in the activity for the child to participate musically – to respond and contribute.
- *Modelling*
  - adult showing or performing and children listen, observe. Modelling may be explicit (watch while I show you) or implicit.
- *Performing*
  - adult (or adults) performing musical activities (live or on video) and child observes, listens and absorbs. Often what has been observed resurfaces in later play.

And all these roles may apply in:

- *One-to-one music* (one-to-two or one-to-a-few) – *adult and child*

- as an important part of making and sustaining relationships in 'everyday' situations;
- for soothing;
- as part of care-giving routines;
- to accompany physical activity – knee-bounces, jiggling, dancing;
- listening and responding together (music on television programmes, CDs, song tapes);
- playing instruments together;
- singing together.

- *One-to-'whoever comes' music – adult with clustering children*
  - adults sit on floor ready to initiate music play – with voice, in movement, with sound-makers and instruments;
  - music as a table activity – a song to link with another activity, listening activity set out at a table;
  - music integrated into dance play, puppet play, role play, outdoor large equipment play.
- *Everyone-with-everyone music – whole groups*
  - circle singing times;
  - group-dance and music times;
  - everyone resting while recorded music plays;
  - everyone watching a performance, participating.

Investigating children's involvement

Observation should ask important questions about the nature of children's and adult–child pairs' involvement in musical activity. This is an important dimension to explore, because there can be a tendency for work in music to be dominated by the performer-entertainer, which can leave little room for genuine engagement and full participation on the part of carer–baby, carer–toddler pairs or young children. At the same time, we should remember that some magic moments of absolute, total absorption by children occur when they are transfixed by an adult performer. So being fully engaged in musical activity can include attentive listening and watching.

In Chapter 6 it was stressed how important it is to develop ways of working in music which enable participation by adult and child pairs. And, importantly, work which encourages quality engagement between adult and baby, toddler or young child. The music worker is, in effect, taking a secondary role as facilitator rather than leader. In thinking about this dimension of involvement, it might be useful to look back at the set of observations in Chapter 5 which focused on the children's different ways of participating in a formal, adult-led singing session.

As will have already become clear throughout this book, music's ability to create connections between people means that is a force for relating well and, at the same time, relating well can be a resource for making more music. It is a two-way process and the emphasis may lean either way. So it might be valuable to focus on the quality of engagement between an adult and baby or toddler, or between young children. It depends on the nature and purpose of the musical activity. At the same time, young children may be making music alone. Again, the descriptions of this book have sought to emphasise the ways in which children spontaneously sing, play instruments and dance as part of play.

Observation can focus on whether the children appear to be:

- fully engaged;
- partly engaged;
- differently engaged – not in an expected way;
- not engaged – distracted;
- being coerced into participating (which would count as not engaged).

Then comes the tricky task of deciding on how one can tell. There are some observable signs: a level of focus, of concentration, of persistence, of regular patterns of eye contact (either focused on the objects or focused on the adult, or regularly incorporating both), and regular patterns of body movements to best enable the activity to continue. A method of measuring children's involvement is explained in more detail in a book which accompanies the Effective Early Learning Project (Pascal and Bertram, 1997). This book also describes how investigating children's involvement was used in a number of early years settings to develop the quality of their practice.

Investigating environments for music

Fostering and supporting music with under-fours involves designing contexts in which musical things can happen. While the environments will include adults in varying roles, they also include spaces and places for music, the selection and provision of equipment and how it is set up. Even just looking at how children use the space in a nursery setting can be informative. For example, when tracking spontaneous dance and rhythmical movement in one nursery I found that the children used a circuit in between tables to skip, dance and sing, but that this was the only free movement space they could find. On some days the circuit was inadvertently blocked by a table, and this range of activity closed down completely. Equally, when I observe where musical instruments are set out it is very often in an out-of-the-way corner, in contrast to activities with a literacy or numeracy focus, which occupy central tables. In one nursery we experimented with bringing a small selection of instruments to the table, in a similar way to the playgroup mothers described in Chapter 5, and stationed an adult 'ready to play'. The involvement of the children in playing the instruments changed dramatically because of this new positioning, as did the quality and creativity of their play.

* Where does music play happen – singing play, movement play, instrumental play: in indoor spaces; on tables; on floor, carpet areas; in small rooms; in outside areas?
* Are equipment set-ups to support different kinds of music play provided in any of these places?
* Are the equipment set-ups stimulating music play as expected?

Investigating a specific problem

A specific problem or area of particular concern or interest may surface. One practitioner, for example, decided that the singing circle time in her nursery had become very routine and tired. She set out a number of questions to frame her thinking:

* How do we choose what songs to sing?
* Why do we sing the songs the way we do?
* How do the children participate in the song singing?
* Do they sing – do they not sing? Can we work out why?
* What songs do the children listen to and know? What does this tell us about their musical interests and abilities?
* What are we aiming for when we sing songs?

Investigating the impact of work

Much work in early years music has a built-in aim to generate more musical activity in an everyday, informal way between babies, young children and their carers. Assessing the wider and longer-term impact of work brings its own challenges. For example, one practitioner wanted to find out whether parents and their toddlers were doing more rhymes and singing at home as a result of home–nursery song sacks she had made. With only a few parents involved, she interviewed them but was sceptical about some of their answers. She suspected they were keen to show how well they involved their children in activities at home. She realised that her interviewing had set up a situation in which the parents felt they were being judged. This example is given, not to deter such efforts, but to show that genuine information about the impact of work beyond the setting can be difficult to obtain and that questioning may touch other anxieties.

Methods for researching the impact of work might include:

- questionnaires;
- informal interviews;
- discussion groups;
- diaries – collected as written (in specially provided books), dictaphone or video diaries;
- recordings of activity at home – photographs, cassette, video.

Review and revision

Questioning and collecting information are the first stage. The next is to analyse and develop understandings from the gathered information. These understandings then need to influence the ways of working and designing of environments for music in a regular cycle of questioning, review, revision and planning. Ideally this cycle is mapped out in advance. Such cycles can be formalised into action research. It is usual in action research to have a supervisor, mentor or critical friend with whom particular ideas, difficulties, successes or achievements can be mulled over.

In developing practice it is important to have contact with others in order to learn from them. This may involve creating opportunities:

- to shadow others with experience and expertise;
- to visit and observe work in a range of settings/ages/groupings;

- to hear about best practice;
- to attend further training;
- for dialogue with other professionals who can support a specific need.

Sharing good practice

Disseminating and sharing to wider audiences is important in the process of extending and evolving good practice. The audience may be all the staff from one setting, a conference hall of hundreds or the unknown visitors to a web site. The forms of dissemination can be various, technology allowing even more possibilities:

- exhibitions, poster displays, documentaries of the children's experiences, with photographs and descriptions written from many angles;
- working diaries: field notes with details of observations;
- conference days: presentation of case studies, presentation of overview studies, seminar discussions;
- write-ups: notes, bulletins, articles;
- video and CD recordings;
- multimedia versions with words, pictures and video.

Areas of expertise

Working with under-fours in music is demanding. The following list is a summary of what I see to be the key areas of expertise as arising from the earlier chapters of description and discussion. They cover a range of knowledge and experience in the early years and music. The summary offers a checklist for self-appraisal.

- Knows about the musical abilities of the under-fours and how they progress.
- Is very aware of and values the ways in which the under-fours are musical.
- Can design musical experiences which allow under-fours – or child and carer pairs – to participate fully.
- Ensures that adult-initiated musical activity is appropriate to under-fours' (or child-carer pairs') capabilities and current priorities.

- Is able to play musically in a way which is appropriate to the age of the children and to their carers.
- Is very alert to children's interpersonal-musical signals.
- Caters for the individual and unpredictable ways of participating, the varying needs for security and to explore among the under-fours.
- Makes available appropriate and quality spaces, times, equipment, recorded and live music.
- Models 'being musical'.

Finally

Early childhood practitioners, music professionals specialising in early childhood music and the parents of young children are imaginative and resourceful people who, if they listen and tune in to the under-fours, will find ways to make music happen for the benefit of all. If this book, in some small way, encourages and supports more music among more young children and their closest adults, then that is satisfaction enough.

Appendix
Music with under-fours: the range of musical behaviours

Musical babies

- recognise mother's voice and music at birth
- make fine aural discriminations
- communicate musically with caregivers
- are assisted in emotional and physical regulation by music
- are soothed and settled by lullabies, physical contact and rocking
- are interested and stimulated by play-songs
- can anticipate phrasing of known songs
- enjoy being moved rhythmically
- listen intently to interesting sounds and music
- shake, tap, lift and drop objects to explore sounds they make
- explore their voice with single-syllable sounds

Adults being musical with babies

- communicate musically with babies
- follow and respond sympathetically to babies' lead
- learn to follow babies' rhythms and cues
- use music to assist emotional and physical regulation
- introduce a variety of sound-making objects
- sing songs, play music games as part of everyday music
- introduce vocally rich rhymes and stories, saying them expressively
- play a wide variety of recorded music to listen to, sing to and dance to

Musical toddlers

- become more independent across the range of musical activities
- begin to vocalise freely – solo in play, communicative with others
- participate in play-songs and songs sung to them in individual ways
- start to learn songs and can reproduce them in individual ways
- shake and tap objects/instruments to produce sound with more controlled, fine motor movements
- develop rhythmic, large-body movements and begin to learn controls and co-ordination
- enjoy repeating and transforming short musical ideas
- are aware of the sound of the music from their home culture
- show a range of responses to music being performed, from intent listening to energetic dancing
- imitate the musical actions of others

Adults being musical for toddlers

- respond appropriately to toddlers being spontaneously musical
- sing songs, read rhymes, story-books, with repetitive fragments
- 'contextualise' music-making by integrating it in general play with toys, activities, books, etc.
- make accessible a wide range of appropriate instruments
- provide environments within which children can initiate music, tolerate and allow for musical boisterousness
- allow more independence and a range of ways of participating
- provide opportunities to hear music being performed, live or recorded
- provide opportunities to engage with adult musical activities within their own locality and beyond

Musical pre-school children

- sing spontaneously in a range of different ways, alone and with others
- learn to sing in own vocal range – singing slowly, with quiet dynamic and short phrases
- begin to pitch match, keep in time with and coordinate their musical ideas with others

- can repeat, transform, combine and develop their own or borrowed musical ideas into increasingly complex structures
- learn to control and coordinate whole body and finer body movements, increasing their range of possibilities in dance and playing instruments – at their own pace
- dance spontaneously to recorded/live music
- are 'open-eared' to a wide range of musical styles and knowledgeable about music from their home culture
- can be an audience listener to live music for short periods of time

Adults participating in pre-school children's music

- continue to provide a rich diet of songs, play-songs, music games, vocal-rich rhymes and stories woven into the everyday
- provide equipment and settings for self-initiated music play with voice, instruments and dancing
- listen and observe, tuning in to children's ways of being musical
- respond and play creatively with children in music, allowing them to retain the initiative
- begin to comment and describe
- support children learning to sing songs by providing appropriate learning opportunities
- support children learning to play instruments by modelling
- provide opportunities to hear a variety of recorded and live music representing different styles and cultures
- model using music in everyday life

References

Atterbury, B. and Silcox, L. (1993) 'A comparison of home musical environment and musical aptitude in kindergarten students', *Update* 11 (2): 18–22.

BBC (British Broadcasting Corporation) (2002) Script, *Child of our Time*, BBC-1, 11 July, 9.00 p.m.

Bruner, J. S. and Sherwood, V. (1975) 'Early rule structure: the case of Peekaboo', in J. S. Bruner, A. Jolly and K. Sylva (eds) *Play: its Role in Evolution and Development*. Harmondsworth: Penguin Books.

Byron, R. (1995) 'The ethnomusicology of John Blacking', in R. Byron (ed.) *Music, Culture and Experience: Selected Papers of John Blacking*. Chicago and London: University of Chicago Press.

Caine, J. (1991) 'The effects of music on the selected stress behaviours, weight, caloric and formula intake, and the length of hospital stay of premature and low birth weight neonates in a newborn intensive care unit', *Journal of Music Therapy* 28 (4): 180–92.

Cassidy, J.W. and Standley, J.M. (1995) 'The effect of music listening on the physiological responses of premature infants in the NICU', *Journal of Music Therapy* 32: 208–27.

DeCasper, A. and Fifer, M. (1980) 'Of human bonding: newborns prefer their mothers' voices', *Science* 208: 1174–6.

DfES (Department for Education and Skills) (1999) *Sure Start: a Guide for Trailblazers*. London: DfES.

Edwards, C., Gandini, L. and Forman, G. (eds) (1995) *The Hundred Languages of Children: The Reggio Emilia Approach to Early Childhood Education*. Norwood NJ: Ablex.

Foster, J. and Thompson, C. (1996) *Chanting Rhymes*. Oxford: Oxford University Press.

Gestel, M. van (2002) 'Music on the Lap', presentation for the conference 'Music with People under Three', University of Surrey, Roehampton, 12 October.

Goldschmied, E. and Jackson, S. (1994) *People under Three: Young Children in Day Care*. London: Routledge.

Gorali-Turel, T. (1999) 'Spontaneous Movement Response of Young Children to Musical Stimulation as Indicator of the Hidden Cognitive Process', paper presented at the conference 'Cognitive Processes of Children Engaged in Musical Activity', Urbana IL: School of Music, University of Illinois at Urbana–Champaign, 3–5 June.

Guilmartin, K. K. and Levinowitz, L. M. (1994) 'A Model for enhancing Music Development through the Inclusion of Informed Parents and other Primary Caregivers in early Childhood Music Classes', paper presented at the International Society for Music Education, Early Childhood Commission, seminar 'Vital Connections: Young Children, Adults and Music', Columbia MO University of Missouri-Columbia, 11–15 July.

Jordan-DeCarbo, J. A. and Galliford, J. (2001) 'The effects of a sequential music program on the motor, cognitive, expressive language, social/ emotional, and musical movement abilities of pre-school disadvantaged children', *Early Childhood Connections* 7 (3): 30–42.

Larkin, Veronicah and Suthers, Louie *What will we Play Today?* II, Edlesborough: Brilliant Publications.

Lecanuet, J. P. (1996) 'Prenatal auditory experience', in I. Deliege and J. Sloboda (eds) *Musical Beginnings: Origins and Development of Musical Competence*. Oxford: Oxford University Press.

MacKenzie, K. (2002) 'The Effect of Infant-directed Singing upon Attachment between Adults and Babies: the Role of Intervention', unpublished MA dissertation, Sheffield: Department of Music, University of Sheffield.

Oldfield, A. and Bunce, L. (2001) 'Mummy can play too': short-term music therapy with mothers and young children', *British Journal of Music Therapy* 15 (1): 27–36.

Papousek, H. (1996) 'Musicality in infancy research: biological and cultural origins of early musicality', in I. Deliege and J. Sloboda (eds) *Musical Beginnings: Origins and Development of Musical Competence*. Oxford: Oxford University Press.

Papousek, M. (1996) 'Intuitive parenting: a hidden source of musical stimulation in infancy', in I. Deliege and J. Sloboda (eds) *Musical Beginnings: Origins and Development of Musical Competence*. Oxford: Oxford University Press.

Pascal, C. and Bertram, T. (1997) *Effective Early Learning: Case Studies in Improvement*. London: Paul Chapman.

Polverini-Rey, R. A. (1992) 'Intrauterine Musical Learning: the Soothing Effect on Newborns of a Lullaby learned Prenatally', unpublished doctoral dissertation, Los Angeles: California School of Professional Psychology (quoted in Cassidy and Standley, 1995).

Rauscher, F. H., Shaw, G. L. and Ky, K. N. (1993) 'Music and spatial task performance', *Nature* 365: 611.

Saffran, J. R. and Griepentrog, G. J. (2001) 'Absolute pitch in infant audi-
    tory learning: evidence for developmental reorganisation', *Develop-
    mental Psychology* 37: 74–85.
Shenfield, T., Trehub, S. E. and Nakata, T. (in press) *Psychology of Music*,
    London: Sage Publications.
Spencer, C. (2000) 'Singing to Babies', unpublished dissertation, University
    of Surrey, Roehampton.
Standley, J. and Moore, R. (1995) 'Therapeutic effects of music and
    mother's voice on premature infants', *Pediatric Nursing* 21 (6): 509–12.
Street, A. (2002) 'Mothers' Singing to Babies: Enhancement of a
    Relationship', presentation for the conference 'Music with People under
    Three', University of Surrey, Roehampton, 12 October.
Suthers, L. (2002) 'Music with Toddlers in Day Care', presentation for the
    conference 'Music with People under Three', University of Surrey,
    Roehampton, 12 October.
Thurman, L. (1997) 'Foundations for human self-expression during prenate,
    infant and early childhood development', in L. Thurman and G. W. Welch
    (eds) *Bodymind and Voice: Foundations of Voice Education*. Minnesota
    MN: Voicecare Network.
Trainor, L. J. (1996) 'Infant preferences for infant-directed versus non-
    infant-directed play songs and lullabies', *Infant Behaviour and Develop-
    ment* 19: 83–92.
Trehub, S. E., Bull, D. and Thorpe, L. A. (1984) 'Infants' perception of
    melodies: the role of melodic con tour', *Child Development* 55: 821–30.
Trehub, S. E. and Schellenberg, E. (1993) 'Music: its relevance to infants',
    Annals of Child Development 11: 1–24.
Trehub, S. E. and Trainor, L. J. (1993) 'Listening strategies in infancy: the
    roots of language and musical development', in S. McAdams and E.
    Bigand (eds) *Cognitive Aspects of Human Audition*. London: Oxford
    University Press.
Trehub, S. E. and Trainor, L. J. (1998) 'Singing to infants: lullabies and
    playsongs', *Advances in Infancy Research* 12: 43–77.
Trevarthen, C. (1980) 'The foundations of intersubjectivity: development
    of interpersonal and co-operative understanding in infants', in D. R. Olson
    (ed.) *The Social Foundations of Language and Thought*. New York:
    Norton.
Trevarthen, C. (1995) 'How Children learn before School', paper based on
    a lecture to the BAECE, Newcastle upon Tyne: University of Newcastle
    upon Tyne.
Whipple, J. (2000) 'The effect of parent training in music and multimodal
    stimulation on parent–neonate interactions in the neonatal intensive care
    unit', *Journal of Music Therapy* 37 (4): 250–68.
Whitwell, G. D. (1999) 'The importance of prenatal sounds and music',
    Journal of Prenatal and Perinatal Psychology and Health 13 (3–4):
    255–62.

Wicker, G. (2002) Course work, University of Surrey, Roehampton.

Woodward, S. C., Fresen, J., Harrison, V. C. and Coley, N. (1996) 'The birth of musical language', *Proceedings*, Winchester: Seventh International Seminar of the ISME Early Childhood Commission.

Young, S. (1995) 'Listening to the music of early childhood', *British Journal of Music Education* 12: 51–8.

Young, S. (1999) 'Interpersonal Features of Spontaneous Music-play on Instruments among Three- and Four-year-olds', paper presented at the conference 'Cognitive Processes of Children engaged in Musical Activity', Urbana IL: School of Music, University of Illinois at Urbana–Champaign, 3–5 June.

Young, S. (2000) 'Young Children's Spontaneous Instrumental Music-making in Nursery Settings', unpublished Ph.D. thesis, University of Surrey.

Young, S. and Glover, J. (1998) *Music in the Early Years*. London: Falmer Press.

Index

Lightning Source UK Ltd.
Milton Keynes UK
UKOW06f1658180515

251781UK00005B/265/P

9 780415 287067